UNMASKING THE INNER CRITIC

Lessons for Living an Unconstricted Life

Andrew Lang

WISE INK

ISBN 13: 978-1-63489-573-6

Library of Congress Catalog Number has been applied for.
Printed in the United States of America
First Printing: 2022

26 25 24 23 22   5 4 3 2 1

Cover design by Kimberly Glyder
Interior design by Patrick Maloney

Wise Ink Creative Publishing
807 Broadway St. NE
Suite 46
Minneapolis, MN 55413

Companion Course

To help you go deeper with *Unmasking the Inner Critic*, I've created a companion course that includes audio and video versions of the body practices and guided meditations, along with additional content to support you on your journey.

Visit www.AndrewGLang.com/unmasking

Contents

Imagine
if all you had to do
to be beautiful

was to
let the wind dance you
where you stand

as you grow into
the only shape
you ever had.

—James A. Pearson[1]

Introduction

I t began with tears.

I sat in the front row of my childhood church in what I knew to be my family's final service in the community where I had grown up. Ordained in the United Methodist Church, my dad was subject to being reappointed on occasion, whenever the bishop decided a change was to be made. To my knowledge, it's a process somewhat akin to that of a general manager's office in the Major Leagues: a group of advisors (known as district superintendents) and the bishop sitting around a boardroom table, moving pastors' names around on a big whiteboard as if preparing for draft day. This year, we were one of the names on the board.

And so I sat in this familiar, one-hundred-year-old sanctuary, the paint on the walls markedly cleaner and more recently painted than when we first arrived. Now at eighteen, I had spent more than ten years as part of this community, and many of my formative memories had taken place within these walls (even my first kiss, although this might be new information for my family).

As community members walked to the front of the sanctuary, again and again wishing us well and sharing stories from eleven years of friendship and connection, I felt increasingly overwhelmed by the transition that was taking place. One of the final church members to share that morning, Betty, began to cry as she spoke of finding a spiritual home there, a group and community to call her own. She shared what it meant to her to watch our once-young family grow up, seeing my older brother venture off to college, and watching from afar as I chased my baseball dreams. It was when she got to me that I lost it. Her eyes locked on mine and tears began to streak down my face, an impulse I still have to this day whenever I see another person cry.

As the service wrapped up and my tears refused to slow, I found myself being embraced again and again by community members and people I had come to view as elders and family friends. My eyes, scanning across the room, landed on one of the oldest gentlemen in our church striding toward me with determined focus. Dale had been an ever-present figure as I grew up, attending every Sunday service, along with various committee meetings, adult education classes, and church outings. As I played in the corner of church meetings or sprinted across the grass at church potlucks, Dale was invariably meandering around, engaging in small talk with anyone he could. If there was a church event, he was there.

He walked toward me, his long stride slowing as the sea of people began to evaporate, the celebration of our time there moving from the sanctuary to the coffee area. He came up to me, his eyes still locked on mine, and placed a firm hand on my shoulder, uttering a statement I would never forget.

"Men don't cry."

I stood for a moment in shock, not quite sure how to respond, while another church member quickly stepped in and whisked Dale away. In the momentary reprieve from hugs and attention, I felt alone and confused, riddled with questions emerging from an unknown space within me.

Why would he say that to me?

How could someone be so unempathetic?

And most of all—if this is what a lifetime of spiritual development produced, why even bother?

* * *

My moment of disillusionment that day marked a turning point in my years-long process of deconstruction as I investigated my Christian upbringing and began to set aside the parts that no longer worked for me. Spurred by my experience with Dale, I found myself searching for trustworthy guides who would help me become the man I wanted to be as well as someone for whom spirituality was connected to how I lived my life. As a person deeply concerned with the state of our world, I yearned for a spirituality that felt intertwined with my social activism and could help me understand my part to play.

Turning away from some of the defining features of my childhood faith, which included weekly church attendance, never-ending potlucks, and a belief in a god who I saw as male, white, and largely distant, I found myself falling deeper into a contemplative spirituality, one in which the divine was best found in the here and now. I began to read modern spiritual teachers such as Richard Rohr, Christena Cleveland, and Thich Nhat Hanh, as well as mystics like Saint Teresa of Ávila and Kahlil Gibran. Rather than feeling disconnected from my spirituality, I felt as if I were embodying more and more a spirituality that could have a real impact on the world. Rather than leaving everything spiritual behind, I began to ask what healthy spiritual development could look like.

* * *

In my own little way, this is a book offering what I myself have found to be liberating and sustaining in my life, with the hope that it may be a support for others as well. In each chapter, you'll find stories, spiritual teachings, reflection questions, action prompts, and body practices that will help you explore your inner life so that you may engage the outer world from a more empathetic and well-grounded place. As you read, I invite you to linger and pause on any teaching that connects with you, setting the book aside for a while if needed, and taking time to work with it in whatever way works best for you.

(Seriously, please don't read this in one sitting. Grab a pen and a cup of coffee or tea, read for a bit, write all over the pages, but then put it down. This book has been written to be digested over time, with plenty of bathroom breaks in between.)

A few years ago, I had the privilege of attending a conference featuring Zen priest and modern wisdom teacher Reverend angel Kyodo williams. Unlike the other speakers who took the stage that day, she taught from atop a pillow, seated with her legs crossed, appearing perfectly grounded in the present moment. It was one of the first times I ever heard someone speak so clearly and with such a sense of authentic credibility, as if what she was saying was flowing through her from a greater source. Afterward, I spent months reading her books and watching her online talks, seeking to understand how she remained so grounded yet focused while discussing the harms and terrors that exist in our world.

As I listened that day, I found myself sloppily scribbling down words I would hear from her again and again in other venues: "Without inner change, there can be no outer change; without collective change, no change matters." For me, this means that the work of inner excavation, paired with spiritual practices that can hold and embolden it, will only matter if it leads to foundational changes in how we see the world. Spiritual development, in whatever form it takes, will only matter if our actions become an outpouring of love that touches and impacts the world around us at personal, communal, and societal levels. Ultimately, our choice to engage the inner life is just the beginning of sustainable activism, a practice in building capacity for the collective work that lies ahead.

CHAPTER ONE

The Spring and the Stream

Growing up in the progressive and leftist circles of Seattle, I was constantly surrounded by people who were active in change-work. Whether it be protesting, political lobbying and organizing, or working in the care industries of teaching, nursing, and social work, almost everyone around me was engaged in our local community. Burnout was everywhere, with few people untouched by it at one point or another. In fact, when I volunteered on a political campaign in my early twenties, the organizers around me would often laugh and joke that it would get them soon, aware they were hurtling toward it at breakneck speed. (Who doesn't like a little bit of dark humor amidst the ridiculousness of life?)

During one of my own seasons of burnout, I stumbled upon the teachings of a Christian mystic named Thomas Merton, who provided me a framework that changed my life and one that will flavor much of this book.

Merton taught that everyone has within them a spring

and a stream. This spring is our inner life, our true self, the essence of who we are. And from this interior spring comes a stream of action—the way we seek justice in our communities and in our world. He said that when our inner life is connected authentically to our outer life, this spring bubbles up from within and overflows outward as a beautiful stream of creative and life-affirming action. In other words, we are able to do what is truly ours to do.

But he said that if our actions aren't connected to our inner life, they become simply a list of to-dos in the face of the overwhelming nature of injustice in the world. And if this is the case, our inner spring, meaning our inner life itself, will become stagnant without a stream to flow into, no longer bubbling with excited vibrancy. Our inner life, therefore, must be tended to and cared for, just as our actions must be authentically connected to that deep space within us.

This teaching, especially when combined with the words of Rev. williams, calls us toward a form of sustainable activism in our communities, one in which our inner life is nurtured and intimately connected to the justice-seeking actions we take in the world. No matter how large or small the action may be, this form of activism finds its essence not in reaction to the crises of the moment, of which there will always be many, but in the spiritual understanding of our own shared and inherent dignity as human beings.

ILLUSIONS + CONSTRICTIONS

According to Merton, the streams of our activism dry up if they lose contact with the spring of our inner lives. Therefore, it makes sense that we would start making more of an effort to get to know our inner lives and the negative self-narratives many of us feel!

When I was young, my parents told me the Tooth Fairy was real. It led me to believe I lived in a magical world, one filled with fairies and some form of strange, twisted economy whereby my teeth could be purchased without my consent, but only in the dead of night. It was an illusion created and birthed unto me, regardless of my desire for it, designed to be discarded with age. When the moment of disillusionment came and I awoke to find my dad sneakily trying to make the extraction from underneath my head-covered pillow, I was ready to let this fairly harmless illusion go.

But not all illusions we hold are harmless; in fact, most of them are inherently dangerous because they alter the way we perceive reality. Each of us is impacted by the continuation, maintenance, and perpetuation of cultural illusions like meritocracy, racism, patriarchy, and heteronormativity; these illusions shape the realities we exist within and how we interact with the world.

When we experience this imperfect world, no matter our position within it and with all the illusions it foists upon us, none of us come away unscarred. We respond by creating further illusions of our own about who we are, ones that can be confirmed again and again by the world outside us as well as within. These illusions we create for ourselves can press inward upon us, constricting us more and more forcefully through the years, until we walk down the street as old curmudgeons, projecting the impacts of our illusions upon others around us.

If you're anything like me, I bet you're quite innovative in the ways you've created your own illusions and narratives; we humans seem to be really good at this! There always seems to be a new way to forget the beautiful possibility born within each of us, a new narrative to create, unburdening us of our inherent dignity and divinity. And while this personal inner critic always seems to be designing new stories that hold us in fear, I would like to invite us to focus on nine specific inner narratives, which I will refer to from here on as constrictions. I'm sure each of us will find at least one that resonates in our own lives.

I am not good enough.

I am not important.

I am not lovable.

I am alone.

I am worthless.

I am not in control.

I am not free.

I am my trauma.

I do not know who I am.

These are *brutal.* And yet, who among us hasn't felt one of these constrictions at some point? When the world shows itself to be imperfect, it is an almost universal truth that we will create narratives of that imperfection within ourselves.

Reflection Questions

Which of these constrictions resonates most within this season of your life?

_____

_____

_____

_____

_____

_____

What does that constriction feel like in your body? Where do you feel it most? How often are you aware of that bodily experience?

_____

_____

_____

_____

_____

_____

Dr. Barbara Holmes speaks to this when she teaches about how we develop and use language. She says that as we interact with the world, the language we use and the stories we tell further construct the world we experience. She gives the example of the word "super-predator," which was made popular by politicians in the 1990s to stir up racist hysteria against teenagers of color. When this word was invented and weaponized publicly, it helped to construct a worldview for white voters of reckless, senseless danger. The world many came to see was developed by the words they were fed.[2]

In the same way, the beliefs we develop over time often further construct the world we experience. When we give ourselves to the belief, experienced or not, that "I am not lovable," our brains will look for every example of evidence it can find. What possibly started as an event where love was lacking (perhaps love from a parent, caregiver, or friend) becomes codified into the very lens through which we see the world.

In response to these constrictions within us, even if they are unexamined and unknown to us at the time, we often go about our lives creating masks for ourselves that can protect us from the impact of those very constrictions. Unfortunately, these masks often distance us even further from our deeper selves.

In her book, *Mindful Silence*, Phileena Nikole shares

that "in our attempts to self-protect and be happy, we end up yearning for that which cannot ultimately satisfy." We mistake our outward personality for our inward personhood and our inherent dignity. And worse, we become known and possibly even respected for the masks we wear, making it all the more difficult to take them off. Nikole writes that wearing these masks is "like drinking a glass of saltwater when you're thirsty. At first it satiates, but then it leaves you sick," until you can't help but seek something more.[3]

Reflection Question

Consider the constriction you resonated with in the previous reflection activity. What masks have you created for yourself to protect against, avoid, or ignore its presence in you?

_____

_____

_____

_____

Eventually, life with these constrictions will lead us toward either liberation from them or mental, emotional, spiritual, and physical burial under them. And while this might feel like an overly dualistic generalization, I don't believe it's an overstatement. Father Richard Rohr, one of the most influential teachers I've had in my life, often likes to say, "If we do not transform our pain, we will most assuredly transmit it." It is my hope that the voices, questions, and body practices in this book can be a helpful guide for us as we examine our constrictions, transforming the ways we relate to ourselves and the ways we engage the world around us.

WISDOM TEACHERS

Not long after my interaction with Dale, I began to read and listen to spiritual teachers who offered an approach to spirituality that began to transform my view of the world and heal many of the wounds and frustrations I carried from organized religion. This approach, known as the Perennial Tradition, recognizes the common spiritual themes and experiences that exist throughout the world's major religions, serving as an undercurrent, constantly flowing underneath the words, flags, dress, and customs of the different religions, pointing us to a deeper understanding of universal truths.

Instead of focusing on what differentiates religions from each either, this approach to spirituality and religion centers on the common wisdom, the common spiritual truths, found in all of them. Jeffrey Moses shares that "when their inherent similarities are revealed, the collected wisdom of the world's religions shows a profound 'Oneness' of the human spirit."[4] Or, to borrow a phrase from my favorite band, Birdtalker, the Perennial Tradition affirms that "we are one wind distracted by our different sails."[5]

The wisdom teachers found in this book all speak to the universality of human dignity inherent within each of us. Some are priests and nuns and some are therapists and trauma specialists. Some are poets while others are philosophers. Many are still living and many are now deceased. Each and every one of them is an elder, someone who has walked their path, learned what it means to be fully human, and sought in their own way to pass along their experiential learning.

SPHERES OF INFLUENCE

As you engage with each of the constrictions explored in this book, I invite you to remember Rev. angel Kyodo williams's teaching: "Without inner change, there can be no outer change; without collective change, no change matters." Everything in this book is intended to serve a twofold purpose, helping to guide us into our inner lives so that we may go outward into our world with the capacity to heal our lives and those around us.

Oftentimes, books like this one can be used as individual "self-help," reduced to a collection of feel-good practices or what Thomas Keating called "high-class tranquilizers." (The man had a way with words.) While comforting, this emphasis on individual growth inhibits our capacities for engaging in outer and collective change.

To help remedy this, let's take a moment to think about our own local contexts. Each of us has spheres of influence in which we can cause real and meaningful change; these are areas in our lives where our opinions and voices might carry some weight within relationships we already have. On a personal level, this might include conversations with our family members, individual friends, and friend groups. In our communities, this might include our workplaces, faith communities, groups we're members of, and boards we sit on. And on a societal level, this can include ways in which we interact relationally with our political and economic structures: advocating, protesting with others, organizing or participating in boycotts, and social justice volunteering. For some of us, we can easily identify spheres of influence at each of these levels; for others, it might be more difficult and point to an area in which we can grow.

Using the space below, think about and label one sphere of influence at each level. In what areas of your life do your opinions and voice carry weight? Who is in those spheres? Who are people in your life with whom engaging in conversation might impact their thinking? In what ways do you currently interact relationally with the broader society through political and economic structures?

If you struggle to come up with one for each level, feel free to leave it blank for now and fill it in later if something comes to you! If you think of more than one for each level, try to focus on the sphere where using your voice can lead to the most impact.

For an example of this activity, visit the companion course.

PERSONAL

What is one sphere of influence you have at this level?

_____

_____

_____

Who is in this sphere?

_____

_____

_____

How might your voice have an impact in this space?

_____

_____

_____

COMMUNITY

What is one sphere of influence you have at this level?

_____

_____

_____

Who is in this sphere?

_____

_____

_____

How might your voice have an impact in this space?

_____

_____

_____

SOCIETAL

What is one sphere of influence you have at this level?

_____

_____

_____

Who is in this sphere?

_____

_____

_____

How might your voice have an impact in this space?

_____

_____

_____

By focusing our change-work on our spheres of influence, we maximize our possible impact, but more importantly, we ensure that our actions are rooted primarily in relationships. In the midst of relationships is where the inner work we do can flow most authentically into the outer work of our lives. Throughout this book, I will ask you to return to these spheres and think about how you can engage them meaningfully.

As we name and begin to work with the constrictions so many of us carry each day in our bodies and minds, I trust that these stories, teachings, questions, and practices will be both comforting and challenging guides, providing us language and encouragement as we excavate the spirit within us and journey into the world in embodied and transformed ways.

CHAPTER TWO

Constriction I: I am not good enough.

Before you keep reading, pause for a moment. As we begin our exploration of these inner constrictions, take some time to sit with the following reflection questions. I know you might want to power through, but seriously, give yourself permission to slow down and spend some time on this. And if journaling isn't your thing, go ahead and take a long walk as you work with the questions.

Reflection Questions

Think back over the past five years of your life to a time when you felt like you weren't good enough. What did it feel like in your body?

_____

_____

_____

_____

_____

_____

When in your life did this constriction first begin to develop within you? Without judgment, try to name who and what led to its development.

_____

_____

_____

_____

_____

_____

All constrictions are born in us from some form of traumatic event or pattern of experiences. Somewhere, somehow in our lives, we were told something, were treated in a specific way, or saw something that led to the formation of these inner narratives in our own minds and bodies. This is often how trauma works. Certain experiences linger in our muscles and our memory until we morph them into a truth we tell ourselves, a self-narrative built on scars and cloaked in a mask we can use to protect us.

Growing up the son of a pastor, this constriction formed in me quite young. Under the ever-watchful eyes of the elders of the church, I grew to understand there were certain expectations, often unsaid, placed upon me. I remember with vivid detail the day I wore my baseball hat in the fellowship room and was met with an older community member forcefully scolding me to "*never* wear a hat in God's house!" (My shoulder muscles still clench up when I think of this.) I learned quickly how to act in front of such people, creating a public personality for myself in which I could be seen as morally acceptable, easy to talk with, a fixer of problems, and an all-around "good kid." The expectations that were placed upon me became internalized and, much like a pressure cooker, I created and became filled with more and more intense expectations for myself. Outwardly, I was humorous and playful, and I leaned heavily on the charisma that came from feeling like I was in a fishbowl. Inwardly, I beat myself up for every missed opportunity to say or do something that would prove I was as good as I wanted to be.

When we believe, as I have throughout my life, that we are simply not good enough, it almost always comes from some experience of failing to live up to expectations, placing a hero on an unreachable pedestal, or stacking our "goodness" against an unachievable goal. While all of these happen to most of us (who hasn't fallen short of an expectation?), there are some of us for whom the healing process wasn't fulfilled in an ideal timespan. We internalized the failing or the feeling of non-goodness and began to write our narrative. Still to this day, our bodies may constrict with the fear of failure and hold an ever-present tension in our shoulders, upper or lower back, or hands well into and throughout our adulthood.

For some, this constriction has been created by religious institutional harm and trauma, often at young ages. The church knows a thing or two about helping people to feel less than glorious about themselves, slinging the words "sin" and "repentance" like darts until their souls might feel utterly shattered. There seems to be so often a cultural forgetfulness within the Christian community about how this universe was created; in the Hebrew oral tradition that formed the developing Jewish scriptures and then the Christian scriptures, God created all that is and named it good. In fact, God said it was good five times before looking at all of creation and proclaiming it was *very* good! Matthew Fox refers to this as our "original blessing."[6] How could we have ever been taught anything less?

A few years ago, I was walking in a park near my house in Tacoma when I experienced a moment of expansion, an awe-inducing instance of clarity that allowed for this constriction to temporarily recede into the background of my life's story. As I stepped slowly along one of the park's many trails, coffee cup in hand as it typically is, I found my attention landing on an old, mangled tree up ahead of me. Its trunk twisted and gnarled, bumps and indents lining it like pockmarks, it seemed strangely out of place in the forested park.

Pausing about an arm's length from the tree, I stared up into its branches, each one swaying in the mild breeze and covered in beautiful green leaves. While the old trunk itself seemed to have experienced no shortage of physical trauma, the leaves were still growing and the branches still danced in the wind. Standing tall in the forest, a unique manifestation amidst the broader "family of things," as the late poet Mary Oliver liked to say, this tree was a reminder for me of our imperfect good-enoughness.

I remember standing at the base of the tree as, for the first time in my life, I experienced what I can now recognize as a brief yet powerful instance of self-love. I knew in that moment, in the presence of all the trees and the little critters and the bushes and the mushrooms (which, I assure you, I had not consumed), that I was wonderfully and imperfectly good enough. I could feel myself shedding my beliefs about needing to prove myself, letting go of old demands to be "the good kid," and releasing the tension I had been holding deep in the muscles of my body. My shoulders unclenched themselves and I just stood, almost certainly with a goofy smile, as I looked up the tree's imperfect trunk into its beautiful canopy of leaves.

This is just one example of how nature has played the role of spiritual teacher for me; perhaps you've had similar experiences out in the forests or by the waters. There is a majesty in the way the beauty of nature so often evades and avoids the shields of our making, flowing sneakily past our defense systems and piercing us through our souls. The mystic Rumi says we have a "void in our soul, waiting to be filled," and I know of nothing that invites me into this soul space quite like taking a long walk through a forest or along a bubbling stream on a sunny day. In these kinds of spaces, we can learn again to breathe deep into our bellies, reclaiming a posture of openness, curiosity, and inherent goodness. This reclamation, which is an act of expansion, can feel like a great bear hug, allowing our bodies to lay down the shame and guilt we have placed upon them, freeing them to love exactly what is theirs to love.

Reflection Question

In what ways have you had a closed-off or non-curious posture in your life? How does this show up in your interactions with the world around you? What might it feel like to reclaim a posture of openness, curiosity, and inherent goodness?

_____

_____

_____

_____

_____

_____

Obviously, this constriction, once developed, does not go away easily; despite my momentary expansion in the park, I quickly found myself returning to my status quo not long after. Because the belief that we are not good enough can show up in every aspect of our lives, it operates less like a knot to be worked out of the muscle and more like a web of interwoven spiritual, emotional, mental, and physical knots. Various wisdom teachers, including Mary Oliver and the storytellers of the Hebrew scriptures, have spoken directly to this constriction specifically because of how difficult it is to transcend.

One of the prevailing insights from various spiritual and wisdom traditions is that our expansion is directly connected with how well we are able to modify the posture in which we experience the world. If we approach the world with a closed-off posture of negativity and judgment, we will experience the events of our lives through the lens of victimhood, always feeling as if the world is being done to us. In each moment of perceived failure or not-good-enoughness, we will close in on ourselves, internalizing the momentary emotions connected to it. However, if we are able to change our posture in the world to being nonjudgmental, open, and allowing, we can learn to experience all of these moments with grace and kindness, accepting them as they are and growing through them. As I say in my workshops, this change in posture does nothing to stop pain and problems, but it does everything to shape how we respond to them.

Buddhist nun Pema Chodron teaches us the importance of this change in posture when she implores us to "fail, fail again, fail better," meaning that through each perceived failing, if we are open to the moment, we can learn from it.[7] In this way, she shows us that the way forward must be through the constriction, intentionally shifting our response to the small, daily instances of imperfection. By doing this, we not only shift how we see the world, but we begin to build capacity to be gentler and kinder with ourselves and others. These small changes can create patterns that, when repeated, work to slowly break down the knots interwoven within us, healing us from the inside.

Reflection Question

As you encounter small, daily instances of imperfection this week, what can you say to yourself in the moment to open your posture, viewing the moment and yourself without judgment or shame?

There is an old story I was told years ago in which a woman is said to have come to a monastery, asking the abbot what the monks did every day. After pausing for a moment, the abbot replied simply, "We fall down, get up, fall down, get up, over and over again." There is a trust in the repetition of the ordinary, that when done intentionally, these daily acts of mindful resilience might allow for an opening to something greater.

It seems that expansion will never be possible with willpower alone. Just as the myth of the self-made man is just that, so too is the idea that healing can happen in an instant or in isolation. If we attempt it (and most of us will try at least once), it'll simply end in another experience of being not quite good enough. Instead, expansion from this constriction requires us to open our posture and accept our own faults and failings in the small moments, retraining our mind and body to interact with ourselves and the world in a way that is honoring and affirming, allowing everything to be imperfect and yet still good enough.

ACTION PROMPT

In which of your spheres of influence can you practice having an open posture? Over the next week or two, how will you look for opportunities to create positive change? Next to each sphere, write one specific form this will take.

Sphere: _____

How: _____

_____

_____

Sphere: _____

How: _____

_____

_____

Sphere: _____

How: _____

_____

_____

BODY PRACTICE: RIGHT-SIZING PRACTICE

Many of us have been taught by our society and those around us to shrink down and make ourselves smaller for the comfort of others. Still others of us have been taught to make ourselves larger than we perhaps ought to be, inhibiting others from taking up their own space. This body practice, which I refer to as the Right-Sizing Practice, is all about giving our body permission to take up the space it deserves (to right-size), whether that's more or less than it usually does in the world.

Find yourself five to ten minutes during your day when you can dedicate all of your intention and attention to this practice.

Standing with about five feet of space all around you, find an equilibrium stance with your feet comfortably resting on the floor and your arms to your sides.

Slowly begin to reach upward and outward with your arms, letting your upper body become as large as it can be. If it helps, you can also move your feet further apart, expanding the space they are taking up as well.

Lengthen and widen your body to its fullest, most expansive-feeling limit, without pushing yourself too far. This should feel like a comfortable, full-body stretch. Spend some time in this position, simply breathing.

Feel what it feels like to fully expand your body. What does it feel like in your hands, shoulders, chest, hips, and legs? How does it impact your breathing?

Now, slowly shrink your body back down to your equilibrium stance and, without stopping, begin to constrict your body even further.

Feel your back bending and your arms caving in and folding into your chest. Let your head and neck turn downward as your knees bend.

Allow your body to become as small as it can, taking up the least amount of space possible. Once again, this should feel like a comfortable, painless, full-body stretch. Again, spend some time in this position as you breathe.

Take some time to feel what it feels like to fully constrict your body. What does it feel like in your hands, shoulders, chest, hips, and legs? How does it impact your breathing?

Now, slowly expand your body back to its equilibrium stance. Take a few breaths, noticing how your body feels.

Repeat this process several times, spending more time in the stance and position that feels the most soul-enriching.

When you finish, make sure to spend a few moments with gentle breathing, allowing your body to simply be.

For a guided version of this practice, visit the companion course.

CHAPTER THREE

Constriction II:
I am not important.

As we begin our work in understanding this constriction, I invite you to enter this chapter through your imagination.

Picture yourself walking through a large clothing store or shopping mall. All around you are signs boasting big sales, images flashing continuously across various screens, and mannequins looking at you with faces that combine lifeless apathy with vague positivity. As you move throughout the store, the air perfumed by that ever-present smell of clothing and dust, you are again and again faced with sale signs, bargain-priced deals, and all manner of verbiage telling you how much better you'll be if you just get that nice, new pair of boat shoes.

Settling into a soft, buttery faux-leather chair, you take out your phone and begin to flip through various apps. You begin doom-scrolling through the latest news of the day before moving on to Instagram, where you are now bombarded by digital marketing, advertising even more products that will make you more beautiful, better at your job, more productive, and most importantly, the best you that "you" can be. The targeted advertising, catered impeccably to your unique tastes and desires, makes it so clear that you are important to the world. And if you have just a few more things, everyone else will notice.

Despite this, many of us hold inner narratives that seem to play on repeat, informing us again and again that we are, in fact, not important at all. The devastating result of perceived slights from others and the actions of those from whom we seek approval, this constriction can tighten within us, souring the view we have of ourselves. This constriction may be experienced intuitively as a contradiction, a feeling of confusion around our own value.

In my own life, the experience of this constriction often involves an active discomfort with acknowledgment and affirmation. When recognized publicly, I can feel my body filling with frantic energy as I shy away, retreating into the background, more comfortable with being seen as a role player. I have often believed that nobody wants to see me because I'm not important, and therefore can be of best use to others if I stay behind the scenes. The messages of marketers preaching my importance never seems to quite balance out the harm experienced from the opposing, internalized messages.

Reflection Question

Think of a time when you felt like you were unimportant. What was happening in that moment? What did it feel like in your body?

_____

_____

_____

_____

_____

_____

I wonder often how high levels of stress, anxiety, and depression in our society, especially within our young people, are a result of this felt contradiction. As a high school teacher, I'm aware that many of my students experience traumas at home and at school that reinforce this pervasive sense of unimportance no matter where they are. And yet, these same students also seem to instinctually know the sense of importance sold by marketing agencies is a hollow promise. This intuitive knowledge shows itself in their amazing knack for sniffing out BS and recognizing the real desire for profit driving the motivations of the business world.

At a deep level, I think they also recognize a truth for all of us: the parts of ourselves marketers are advertising to aren't the important parts of ourselves. The parts of ourselves that can be purchased by a few punchy ad-lines and colorful marketing *aren't* important. And because of this, we need to seek out the parts of ourselves that are. Although advertising agencies will continue to spend their energy, money, and time selling this hollow importance to our surface-level sense of self, there's another part of ourselves that is deeper and more valuable, one that is singing out to us, though we may not recognize or be able to name it.

Howard Thurman, a Christian minister, theologian, and spiritual mentor to Martin Luther King Jr., refers to this as the "sound of the genuine" emanating up from within us. We can hear it, sometimes breaking through the noise of life in the *aha* moments and sometimes only within our quiet spaces, but it is always strumming within us, trying to lead us deeper into the depths of who we truly are. If we're able to pause and listen, we might hear this intimate sound coming up from within us through our intuition, our creativity, and our passion. (For those of you who are artists, I bet you know this feeling! The sound of the genuine often leads us into "being in the flow," as our bodies, minds, and souls come together to create something beautiful.)

In short, the sound of the genuine is our internal beckoning call, ushering us toward the part of ourselves that holds our true importance, the part of ourselves that existed before the creation of our protective identity masks and our personas, and will exist after the world strips each part of our false protections away. It is the core of our being and, as James Finley calls it, that which is "invincibly precious" within us.

Reflection Questions

In what context have you ever experienced the sound of the genuine emanating from within you? What thoughts, insights, or bodily sensations occurred within you?

_____

_____

_____

_____

_____

_____

How would you walk with or toward another if you truly believed you were both important in the cores of your being? How would your actions change?

_____

_____

_____

_____

_____

_____

It is through this sound of the genuine that our true self communicates with us, often in silent whispers and uncomfortable questions. It issues a sound that calls us to its realness and invites us to dig deeper for a more authentic way of living, a more authentic way of being ourselves. Mirabai Starr writes to each of us when she says, "Yes, you are worthy of art making. Dispense with the hierarchy in your head that silences your own creative voice . . . It is not only your birthright to create, it is your true nature. The world will be healed when you take up your brush and shake your body and sing your heart out."[8]

It is true that I am not important and yet equally true that I am. In each of us resides this essential and inherent dignity, unique and indestructible, an inner force that cannot be taken from us. While the world competes for the attentions of the parts of ourselves that thrive on recognition, this true self lingers in our depths, quietly singing and waiting to be heard. By turning our attention inward and listening for the sound of the genuine in ourselves, we are able to reconnect with this core essence of our humanity and begin to root our lives there. In listening for what might bring us alive, we may begin to let go of our fear that the parts of ourselves we have long built up and shown off are "not important" and rather begin to build a better home for ourselves in the parts that most certainly are.

Mirabai Starr hits on something so essential in her teaching that it bears repeating: "It is not only your birthright to create, it is your true nature." For those of us who are perplexed by this idea of listening for the sound of the genuine inside ourselves, we should look no further than the creative parts of our lives. Often, it is when we are designing, dancing, or creating that our true self is most likely to be heard. The act of pausing and directing our intention to the practice of allowing whatever comes to come is a great way of listening to ourselves and reclaiming the truth of our inherent importance! All creativity is a practice of allowing something mysterious and new to take form from our being, after all. For some of us, this takes the form of making something physical through traditional or modern arts forms, but for some of us it can be a moment of getting lost in a song and singing our hearts out! (Personally, singing in the shower is one of my most treasured creative outlets.) Each of us has the potential to come into contact with our creative nature. I invite you to pause reading, turn on some of your favorite music, grab a piece of paper, and start doodling. My bet is that before long, you'll be lost in the music or in whatever is taking shape on your page!

That said, there are other ways to shift our attention and begin to listen to the sound of the genuine emanating from within us. If dancing, singing, and creating don't seem to fit your style, I invite you to embrace the ancient practices of silence and solitude. Find yourself a day when you can disappear for a few hours from all responsibilities, friends, and family, instead dedicating the day to exploring your interior landscape. For me, I do this best when I'm in nature, so I will often find myself on Saturdays looking out at the Puget Sound or walking along one of the many Pacific Northwest tree-covered trails. In the silences and retreat from our norm, there become fewer distractions competing for our attention. In this space, we can better listen for whatever is in us desiring to be heard, becoming more fluent in the language of our true self. If this sounds appealing to you, the Body Practice at the end of the chapter might be perfect for you!

Whether it be through creativity for creativity's sake or through practices of silence and solitude, the work of expansion is the work of listening and settling into our "true nature," as Starr calls it. It is this interplay between outward attention and inward listening that brings bubbling up within us our capacity to hear the sound of the genuine in ourselves.

ACTION PROMPT

Who is one person in your personal or community spheres of influence who you often have difficulty with that you might interact with this week? After you identify the sphere of influence they're in and who they are, brainstorm how you might listen for the sound of the genuine emanating from within them. Then, list how you might respond to them from that place within you.

Sphere: _____

Who: _____

How: _____

_____

_____

_____

_____

_____

BODY PRACTICE: NATURE WALK

Find an hour or so in your schedule when you can go to your nearest park, arboretum, or beach. If you can, leave your phone behind at home or in the car; this practice works best if there is no temptation to use any electronics.

Before you begin, take a moment to stand or sit in stillness. Draw your attention to the breeze, the sun on your skin, the sounds around you, and your body against the earth. In these one or two minutes, breathe deeply and simply place your attention on the sounds and smells around you.

For the first five minutes of your walk, be mindful of your pace and how your feet are coming into contact with the ground. Walk slowly enough that you can pay attention to the wonderful world of nature around you. Use this time to ground yourself in nature, setting aside all other thoughts and to-do items for the moment.

As you become comfortable walking, start to intentionally listen for the sound of the genuine coming from all around you. What is the sound of the genuine that emanates from deep inside the birds, from the movement of the trees, from the land creatures? In witnessing them, how are you becoming aware of the sound of the genuine coming up from within you? How is the sound of the genuine in them connecting with and similar to the sound of the genuine in you? If it feels right, feel free to stop and pause at any time, simply observing and experiencing the natural world around you.

Feel free to wander, zigzag, pause, or explore whatever draws your attention; above all else, take your time. Notice how you are part of the landscape; come into contact with your importance in this moment.

When you reach your ending point, take another moment similar to how you started. Pause in the stillness, listening to the world around you, and express your gratitude for the natural world, which you are a part of!

CHAPTER FOUR

Constriction III:
I am not lovable.

When I was fresh out of college, I had a good friend named Lauren. I would often spend time with her and her partner out at the bars or at cozy breakfast spots on Saturday mornings. She had a curious tendency to consistently ask her partner, "Do you love me?" Never mind they had been together for some time and that for the most part, everyone around them knew the answer that would come. Even Lauren knew the answer; this wasn't a question seeking a rational response, but rather an inquiry seeking continued confirmation of what she already knew, which is why she would always ask it in a cutesy, bashful way, with a big smile on her face or a bad attempt at a pouty face. Sometimes she would even throw an extra "even" in there just for effect. ("Do you *even* love me?")

What most of us saw as an attempt at humor and a fishing expedition for compliments and verbal praise, Lauren later shared was a deep yearning to make sure she wasn't losing the person closest to her. It was a coping mechanism, one she habituated into her life to deal with trauma from her childhood.

When she was young, Lauren and her siblings had what outwardly looked like a wonderful, safe, suburban life. Both her parents worked during the day and the kids were all kept busy playing sports or participating in after school clubs. When they got home, they ate together and talked about their days. There was only one thing missing: the participation and presence of Lauren's father. A devoted worker, he would choose to spend long hours at the office, coming home only to rest before sprinting off to his next thing, whether it be more work or one of his many side projects. Keeping busy was his own way of dealing with the constrictions he was carrying.

But to Lauren (and much of the family), they simply witnessed his absence. Lauren grew up hardly knowing her father, and what she did know of him, she certainly didn't want to emulate. She came to resent him when he was home, assuming he was still working inside his mind. Even when he was present, he didn't ever seem *present*.

As Lauren grew up, she internalized this absence as rejection. No matter how much love her mother showed her, Lauren still carried the weight of having a father who was missing in action. When she began college, she started to visit with a therapist to help with stress and soon began to unpack the feelings she was carrying around love, rejection, and, ultimately, her relationship with her father. She had made the decision that progress needed to be made, in her at least, to heal some of the trauma that had been caused.

Reflection Question

What did you learn about love from your family or from others who were important to you? How has this shown up in your relationships with others and yourself?

_____

_____

_____

_____

_____

_____

This story obviously isn't unique in a culture that values productivity over relationships. Perhaps someone you know, or yourself, has a similar tale to tell: the internalized rejection from someone close, the breakdown and consequences of a parent-child relationship, the fear caused by events witnessed as a child. And while it may be a cliché, it doesn't stop this trauma from being deeply true in so many of our lives.

But Lauren's consistent questioning of her partner—"Do you love me?"—wasn't only fueled by her childhood trauma. That would be an incomplete and damaging understanding of how behavior works. She had also been deeply influenced by a culture that treats love as something to be shown through Valentine's Day gestures, replete with chocolate roses, declarations of never-ending companionship, and a Hallmark card (and possibly a dramatic duel with another potential suitor).

And while so many of us have been taught to romanticize this unrealistic form of romantic love between partners, we have also been taught to romanticize an equally unrealistic form of parental love, one that is unconditional and can survive all things. While this may certainly be true for some parent-child relationships, it is hardly the lived experience of most children, many of whom grow up in families where one or both parents have left, divorce or separation is unavoidably present, or, like Lauren's story, one or both parents have simply checked out.

I want to note here that regardless of the actual reasons for these things happening, children see these events through their own lenses and understandings of the world. Even if there exist very good reasons for divorce or distance, many children will still process that experience of loss as a form of rejection or simply as a void to be filled.

Realistic or not, we've been fed these images of romantic love and unconditional love since childhood here in our Western culture. These images are powerful and speak deeply into our psyche of desire and fulfillment; they sell movies, cards, books, and any sort of thing that can be sold and given as a Christmas present. (Every year when I see Christmas car commercials, I wonder who buys and gives a car to their partner as a Christmas gift; I've never met one of those people.)

The more we have internalized these images as "the norm," the more we seek to achieve them in our lives. We search through Tinder and OKCupid profiles to find that elusive and perfect romantic love or spend hours upon hours at our therapist's office working to repair our relationships with our parents. And the more we look to fill this void we feel with these different forms of unrealistic love, the tighter this constriction becomes in us as we ask, "Do you love me?"

Reflection Question

What is your current relationship with love? How do you define love, given the way you've experienced it in your life?

_____

_____

_____

_____

_____

_____

As a society, we've turned love into a commodity to be given and taken away, which sells well, creating ever-dependent consumers, but hides the reality of what love is. Love is not primarily a verb, but rather a noun. It isn't something within a transaction, but rather the foundation for all purpose, relationships, and meaning-making. It is the basis, the lifeblood, of all that is.

In our verbification of love, we have collectively covered up this noun-nature. The constriction of "I am not lovable" comes from a conditioned forgetting of the truth that we *are* love, that each of our existences is love-infused and love-abundant. It isn't a question of whether we receive it from so-and-so or who we choose to give it to; love is our true nature, the energy through which the true self sings its "sound of the genuine." Anything less than the full realization of this truth leaves us operating from our false self, our masked self, filled with constrictions ever tightening within us, searching desperately for something that cannot be given to us, yet exists within us and all around us. We are left grasping for gifts and kind words when what we truly desire is the radiance of love coming from within ourselves and one another.

James Finley often speaks of the "intimate immediacy of love," the constantly present and infinitely close nature of love in all moments. He teaches that love is like a thread, weaving its way beautifully through all of life, connecting everything together. The sun rising in the morning, strangers waving to one another, little critters running around the park—these are all manifestations of love already present in our universe. Our invitation is to become more and more stabilized in our awareness of this thread, seeking to hold onto it without letting go. By remaining in contact with it, our awareness of the ever-present nature of love radically transforms how we see and engage with the world around us.

In other words, we don't need to buy into the commodification and verbification of love. So long as we live and breathe, the way we manifest our energy, our true selves, is the radiation of this love-nature. This is what the mystics and wisdom teachers of all traditions have sought to teach us in their own words, limited by time and culture: love is not a product to be given and received in the same way we would a present. It radiates from deep within our being. And therefore, rather than spend our time searching for others who will declare their companionship for us and call it love, instead seek those whose energy manifests their true love-nature, those who sing the sound of the genuine out loud for the world to experience, and seek to become one of those people.

Coming into contact with our own love-nature is not altogether that different from the process of listening for the sound of the genuine coming from within oneself. Our love-nature is just waiting to be tapped into, whether it be through creative works, silent meditation, or a reflective walk through nature. However, because so many of us have been taught to avoid the act of self-love, we often must traverse added internal barriers in order to recognize the love that is at the depths of our being.

I often think of this internal journey as a two-step process: the first step we must take is to create boundaries that recognize our own needs and value. Many of us who experience this constriction are so hungry for love from others that we give and give and give with the hope that our giving will be reciprocated. When it isn't, we burn out, our physical and emotional lives paying the ultimate sacrifice in the forms of anxiety, stress, sadness, and depression. Therefore, we first need to create boundaries that protect us from giving or pouring out too much of ourselves into another person. The most important words for this step are "I can't do that right now."

In my second year of teaching, I learned this the hard way. In the midst of a school merger, I decided to become one of our union's building representatives in addition to my usual teaching duties. I jumped headfirst into every issue and organizational argument, attempting to fix each problem that arose one by one. For anyone who has been part of an organizational merger, you know where this is going: I burned out quick. Without boundaries that honored my needs, I didn't have the emotional resilience to maintain a healthy life-work balance, and those around me, including myself and my students, suffered because of it.

Once we are able to set these healthy boundaries that can serve us, our capacity to recognize our own love exponentially increases. All of a sudden, when we are no longer pouring out our energy for the comfort of others, we have time and energy to be the recipient of our own care. It is in taking care of ourselves through eating well, finding a sport or exercise we have fun doing, reading books, listening to podcasts, or any number of sustaining activities that we begin to feel the radiation of our own love-nature.

As I was burning out at work, I became depressed, moody, and generally unpleasant to be around; I was, to some extent, like a ship that had lost its rudder. One of my dear friends, knowing I was struggling to stay afloat, invited me to start playing racquetball each week, a sport I only knew through watching old men at the YMCA play as I passed through. I immediately felt like I had found myself again. By engaging my body and entering into a new rhythm, I created space in my life to be *me*. I mentioned this experience in Chapter Two, but it was during this phase of my life that I first came into contact with the feeling of self-love. Walking through that forest, I had this sense of love wash over me and I knew it wasn't from any exterior source; it was my first time ever recognizing that I was worth it, good, and above all else, filled with love. To this day, I cannot fully explain the different factors that prepared me for that moment, but I know that setting boundaries, honoring myself, and learning to enjoy my body again were core parts of it.

Reflection Question

What boundaries do you need to create and maintain in order to best honor yourself?

_____

_____

_____

_____

_____

_____

Moving from constriction to expansion requires us to become aware of our own love-nature inside us and awaken to the existing presence of love in the world around us. In her podcast, *Love. Period.*, Jacqui Lewis is joined by Kaliswa Brewster in a conversation on what Lewis calls "fierce love." She says this is the kind of love that combines the passion of friend-love, the desire of romantic love, and the unconditionality of healthy parental love, emitting from within us a form of love that can be directed both inwardly as self-loving energy and outwardly as justice-seeking passion. Lewis continues, "It's like, do not get between a mama bear and her cub; it's like, I will throw down for you because you're my posse; it's like, I will jump in the streets because George Floyd got murdered . . . [This fierce love] will transform us and change us and stretch us, and I am convinced it has the power that will help our world."[9]

When we awaken to our own love-nature, our capacity to embody this explosive kind of fierce love, we have no choice but to open our eyes to the love-nature in others. We no longer need to ask anyone if they love us because we experience their love radiating in the ways they listen, communicate, create, and care.

ACTION PROMPT

Scenario: You are walking home one afternoon when you see two police officers speaking in what seems like an aggressive tone to a young teenager of color. You observe one or two others on the street, but they do not appear to be aware of the situation.

Resource: Take a few minutes to visit www.ihollaback.org. Review their resources for how to be an active bystander, specifically with this scenario in mind. (*A link to this resource is in the companion course.*)

Brainstorm: Then, brainstorm ways in which you might respond in this situation in a way that affirms the inherent dignity and love-nature of everyone involved, especially the young teenager of color.

_____

_____

_____

_____

BODY PRACTICE:
EXPERIENCING LOVE-NATURE

This is an extremely simple practice that can be used just about anywhere and as often as you need in order to come into contact with your own love-nature.

Sitting or standing, gently place your hand over your heart, skin-to-skin if possible.

Take a few moments to simply feel the heat of your body and the rising and falling of your chest and stomach. Focus on the natural rhythm of your breath as it enters and moves through your body.

After a minute or so, with your attention on your heartspace, say to yourself, "I feel your love." If this feels too far from your current truth, you can also say, "I seek to feel your love."

Spend a few minutes breathing and saying this line from time to time. Try not to create a mantra out of it that you repeat over and over again; simply let it be a reminder, spoken when needed.

As you do this, imagine your heartspace opening up and letting the love that is naturally within you overflow outward. Sit in the experience of abundant love radiating from within you.

When you're ready, slowly let your hand drop from your heart, open your eyes, and take a moment to rest in this experience before moving into the next part of your day.

For a guided version of this practice, visit the companion course.

CHAPTER FIVE

Constriction IV:
I am alone.

The term "alone" took on an entirely new meaning with the advent of the COVID-19 pandemic. Sitting in our apartments, houses, and homes, we learned to say no to seeing friends and family, instead opting to surround ourselves with boxes of disposable facemasks and the largest bottles of hand sanitizer we could find. (If you're like me, you may have also attempted to make your own hand sanitizer. Unlike me, you may have been successful.)

This experience of COVID-19 laid us out bare; on a societal level, it shed further light on the inequities and injustices that lie at the heart of our housing, economic, criminal justice, education, and health systems. On a personal level, it forced many of us to face our own existences in the silence and quietness of our own homes and minds. For so many, it was a time of awakening, both to the world as it is but also to our own inner relationship with ourselves.

Amidst the trauma of self-isolating, friendships-at-a-distance, and lost loved ones, we found ourselves coping with personal and communal questions of purpose, meaning, and possibility. At the beginning of the pandemic, in March 2020, people in cities across the world stepped out onto their porches and balconies to bang pots and pans in honor of those working to save lives in hospitals and clinics. Within a month, neighbors began to step out of their homes where they had been quarantined to host socially-distanced disco parties along the empty streets. When the police murder of George Floyd occurred in May, people of all different races across the United States showed up and spoke up for the humanity of people with Black bodies in a way that hadn't been seen in decades. There was an energy in the early months of the health crisis that exposed the possibility for deep connection-making and justice.

As more months went by and people settled into the new routine of their lives, these events slowly dwindled and many who had been animated about racial justice slipped back into their default way of being. The chorus of pots and pans every evening became mundane, rather than hopeful, and then died away altogether. The socially-distanced discos were replaced by Zoom visits online with people who were already comfortably within our friend groups. Support for the Black Lives Matter movement amongst white Americans fell from 60 percent in June to 45 percent by September, as many people with white bodies once again chose daily comforts over fighting against the inhumane nature of our social systems.[10]

And as we settled into the realities of living through a global pandemic, many also entered fully into unsteady lives of isolation, marked for so many by joblessness, frustration, and a deep sense of aloneness. This was certainly true for me as I came face-to-face with my own heightened levels of anxiety and depression, as so many of us had to. The pandemic did not create this constriction, this sense of being alone in the world, but it certainly created the conditions for the constriction to tighten within our bodies and hide the truth of our connections from us.

Reflection Questions

During the COVID-19 pandemic, how did you experience this constriction of feeling alone? What did it feel like in your body?

_____

_____

_____

_____

_____

_____

What does it feel like in your body when this constriction tightens or loosens?

_____

_____

_____

_____

_____

_____

In 2014, I remember sitting with my family each week as the updated version of Carl Sagan's *Cosmos: A Personal Voyage* was released on TV, this time as *Cosmos: A Spacetime Odyssey*. For those of us who hadn't grown up with Sagan, this show was introducing us to some of the great mysteries of the physical universe, showing us with brilliant animation how complex our reality truly was. Hosted by the venerable Neil deGrasse Tyson, the show was a powerful mixture of great storytelling, clear and well-explained science, and solid animation.

There was one scene in particular, however, that I remember with vivid detail. In the scene, Tyson slowly walks toward the camera and says, in his uniquely comforting voice, "Some claim that evolution is just a theory, as if it were merely an opinion. The theory of evolution—like the theory of gravity—is a scientific fact. Evolution really happened. Accepting our kinship with all life on Earth is not only solid science. In my view, it's also a soaring spiritual experience."[11] He later goes on to share one of his most quoted and unifying insights: that we are each stardust, created from the same chemical compounds and uniquely linked. For me, this scene was akin to a mystical moment; I felt directly and spiritually linked into this mysterious and interconnected universe.

I had a sense that by simply continuing to be alive, I could never be removed from this great web of being, this interdependent universe.

And if that's true for all of us, then we are irrevocably

members of a vast interdependent community of beings, even when we feel all alone! Our individual experiences of what it means to move and operate as human beings are not disconnected from the experiences of those around us, which means even in our silent glances or our momentary sharing of the same space while merging on a highway, we are connected through a mysterious interpersonal reliance. Even when we are physically alone, we are not separated from the neutrons, protons, and electrons communicating with and through us.

The work of letting go and expanding through this constriction lies in our gradual opening to this Reality, as complex and mysterious as it may be. Feeling alone does not only come from a lack of contact or deep connection with other humans, but ultimately from a fragmented view of the universe itself. We can only feel alone when we do not see the trees as our genetic siblings, the water as our body of atomic ancestors, and the animals around us as fellow journeyers. Instead, expansion is the work of opening our eyes so that we can, like St. Francis of Assisi, refer to all members of the universe as our brothers, sisters, and siblings.

Reflection Question

When is a time you've felt connected to the natural world around you or to another person, perhaps whom you've just met?

_____

_____

_____

_____

_____

_____

A few years ago, I participated in an event with about a hundred others, learning skills around community care. As the event was catered to the needs of pastors and lay leaders, mostly from more rural and conservative areas, I was likely the only one in attendance who did not actively belong to a faith community. Because of this, and my assumption of the political makeup of the group, I wasn't sure I belonged here either, and yet, here I was. As an act of self-preservation and protection, I found myself living along the edges of the event room, happy to hug any wall I could find, never without a cup of coffee in hand.

On the second day of the event, I found myself venturing out of the room during a particularly long presentation, feeling out of context and alone. After getting a drink of water and meandering the halls, I returned to my post in the back of the room, where most people couldn't see me leaning against my wall of safety.

I looked around the room, truly noticing for the first time all the people who had dedicated a weekend to be here. Unlike before when my brain had unceremoniously labeled them as "conservatives" and "fundamentalists" (which, looking back, was probably wrong anyway), something new happened for me. For each person that existed in that room, I saw a story and a desire. Something about that person's life had led them to be here, seeking ways to better serve their communities. Despite our potential religious and political differences, we each had a beautiful desire for a better world for our loved ones. In each of us in that room, the sound of the genuine was strumming its unique chords.

It was a revelation for me that broke through my unexamined judgmentalism, seemingly liberating me from yet another illusion I found myself in. I had chosen the isolation of passing judgment because it helped me maintain a sense of superiority, but that shattered in the face of recognizing common humanity. It was true then just as it is now, wherever you are—we each exist in an interconnected universe, our very beings drawn together through a patchwork of stories, experiences, and dreams for the future.

What I experienced on that day is no different from anything we can experience if we pause to look mindfully at the universe we operate within. At the core of our being, we each hold an intimate common ground with all living things, a connectedness that is irremovable and unbound by time and space. This doesn't mean we all have to like each other; it is simply the recognition of our common divinity, humanity, and inherent dignity that changes the shape of our society. We can recognize each other's worth without socially bonding just as we can disagree without dehumanizing. This change in posture toward one another, setting aside the false boundaries of good and bad, in and out, powerfully charges that everyone belongs and that nobody is beyond reconciliation.

In case you need a scientific approach to support this idea of timeless interconnection with others, we are coming to understand more and more through the developing field of epigenetics. Trauma specialist Resmaa Menakem speaks clearly of our connection with our ancestors and descendants, those who have come before us and those who will come after us, when he explains that the experience and impact of trauma codes itself into our genetic material, spreading from "one body to another, like a contagious disease—through families and from generation to generation." Menakem continues that "like trauma, resilience can be passed down from generation to generation" through this process of genetic inheritance.[12] In other words, we're starting to understand on a more holistic level how we are each mysteriously integral to this universe, this timeless community of potential and pain, connected from the genetic to the physical, from the biological to the behavioral.

In this great web of being, nothing and nobody is left to be alone.

ACTION PROMPT

A few years ago, I heard the phrase, "Never take action alone." Pause for a moment and think about the ways in which you interact with the political and economic structures of society, and then look back to the societal spheres of influence you named in Chapter One. Who are one or two people from within your community you might invite to participate with you in your engagement at the societal level? How might you double or triple your impact by not "taking action alone"?

Who: _____

Invitation: _____

_____

_____

_____

_____

BODY PRACTICE: CONNECTION GAZING

Often used in our modern world by couples and romantic partners and rooted in both Hinduism and Buddhism, connection gazing or "eye gazing" is a practice of intention and observation.

For this practice, you'll need an "other." It can be an object, another person, or a living creature from the natural world. I have personally found it can be most powerful with a close friend or with a living organism, such as a majestic tree or beloved pet.

If you're doing this with a partner or friend, recognize first that it might feel awkward. This isn't a typical thing to do! You might want to start with a shorter amount of time, like one to three minutes, and then increase as it becomes comfortable.

Find a place where you can sit comfortably for ten minutes or so, setting a timer if you desire.

With your body oriented toward the "other," breathe deeply and settle your gaze upon them. If doing this with a partner or friend, let each of your gazes be focused on each other's eyes. If you'd like to hold hands or touch, that can also be powerful!

As you breathe, soften your eyes and simply observe them. Try to look beyond their physical manifestation and into their soul/heartspace, seeking connection with them. Maintain your gaze and try not to look away.

Break your gaze when the timer goes off.

CHAPTER SIX

Constriction V: I am worthless.

In the last chapter, I used the word "being" eight times and in a multitude of different ways. I realize that this chapter needs to begin with a bit of an explainer.

In a culture fixated on *doing* and getting things done, *being* often gets forgotten and relegated to the backdrops of our lives. And yet, *being* is our ultimate default as humans; regardless of what we do or complete or achieve, we *are*. The old philosophical statement on human existence put out by René Descartes ("I think, therefore I am") is simply wrong. I *am*, therefore I am. My being speaks for itself.

The Jewish tradition has a beautiful old teaching around this as it relates to the name of God. Historically, the Jewish name for God (Yahweh) has not been permitted to be spoken aloud by Jewish adherents. But in some teachings, the name is allowed to be *breathed*, with "yah" being sounded with the breath on the inhale and "weh" being sounded on the breath during the exhale. In this way, every breath we take becomes both a statement of our being in this world as well as a statement of connection to the divine.

And so, when I speak of our *being* or our *way of being*, or even the *great web of being*, I'm referring to the very nature of our connected existence, underneath and regardless of all the doings we might be engaged with. It was told to me once that the ultimate objective of life is to be in a state of constant "is-ness," which means to be constantly present to the world and ourselves exactly as it is and exactly as who we are. It is this *being* that will change the world.

Unfortunately, our world doesn't care much for *being*, opting more for the work of *doing*. It has more quickly accessible results, is easier to control through incentives, and is much easier to attack with shame, guilt, and judgment, which are always means of control in and of themselves. (Telling someone to "be better" rarely has anything to do with actual *being*, and almost always more to do with actions or behaviors that don't live up to someone else's arbitrary standards.)

We are told that it is through *doing* that the world changes, objectives are met, and happiness will arrive for us. There is little space in our culture for the truth that Evelyn Underhill speaks when she teaches us that "a lot of the road to heaven has to be taken at thirty miles per hour."[13] Instead, those of us in the Western world focus on speeding as fast as we can, telling and retelling narratives that promote climbing corporate ladders, working for the next promotion, achieving at all costs, and constantly pushing ourselves to improve. These narratives assume and depend upon us believing that we are in a state of unnecessary imperfection, one that we can work our way out of if we just *do* enough. So we buy into these narratives and begin to internalize them, first believing we are worth less than we can be, and then, after enough time and energy is spent attempting to prove ourselves, we can come to believe we are simply worthless. This constriction grows within us, cutting off our own ability to see anything other than our own inferiority to those who "have it all figured out."

Reflection Question

In your life, what events or moments have caused you to question your own self-worth? What lessons have you internalized from these experiences?

_____

_____

_____

_____

_____

_____

Many of us feel the void, the inner emptiness, the constriction, and look to the industries that just so happen to profit most off our feelings of worthlessness. We turn to shopping sites and self-help books, social media and Instagram posts beautifully selling a "treat-yo-self" form of self-care as the answer. This culture of *doing* has built unbelievable strength, power, and wealth for companies and industries who know how to best manipulate it.

And not dissimilarly, how many of us have felt this in the spiritual and religious worlds? Much of religion itself, and especially Christianity here in the United States, has been poisonously used to create and then profit off our own lack of self-worth, teaching us that if we only control ourselves more, sacrifice a bit more, or give a bit more, we will climb the steps toward God and inner peace. (In this demand for an impossible perfection, I see a clear connection between the idea of climbing the steps to God and climbing the corporate ladder—two concepts that are intrinsically linked.)

While on retreat recently, a group of friends and I stayed up late talking about our respective upbringings and faith traditions. For the most part, I was the odd one of the group. Having grown up in progressive Christian settings, the stories of their conservative and evangelical backgrounds were mostly foreign to me, placing me firmly in a posture of listening as they unpacked their childhood confusions and what they had been taught.

Of all the topics we discussed, this was most clearly apparent when we got to sexuality. As they shared with grief-filled laughter their stories of purity culture, promise rings, and abstinence-only education, I heard each of them explore the long-lasting impact of the church-based shame and guilt that had been injected into them. Each of their churches, located in towns across the United States, had used sexuality, our natural and biological desire for physical connection, to condemn and control their lives and those of their friends. In other words, sexuality had been violently weaponized to determine their worth.

At first, I just stood back and listened as if I were observing something brand new to me—my upbringing had been nothing like that! In fact, sexuality had barely been mentioned at all in my progressive church, let alone used to parcel out who was good and who was bad.

But then again, that was also a problem.

While I hadn't been subject to purity culture or promise rings, it was quietly implied that sex was meant to be saved for marriage. And while our church liked to fly a pride flag every Sunday, almost everything about my experience of church defaulted to being heteronormative. As the great historian Howard Zinn liked to say, "You can't be neutral on a moving train." In the face of a Christian culture chugging along with a conservative "sex-is-shameful" dynamic, the failure of my progressive upbringing to openly provide a sex-positive theology meant I was also filled with shame and guilt around sex. Without an alternative vision, I was unable to divorce sexuality from the questions of worth attached to it.

Likewise, without an alternative vision for human worthiness in general, many of us are stuck with existential questions of worth in our day-to-day lives. When I'm feeling down or low, this often manifests in a feeling of cosmic insignificance or what I refer to as nihilism-light: a pervading sense of "what's the point?" The mystics, many of whom I refer to in this book as our wisdom teachers, bought into an alternative operating system, one in which *being* made us worthy simply because the divine breathed life into us. The Sufi poet Rumi likens this divine DNA to a candle within us just waiting, without shame or guilt, to be lit ablaze:

> *There is a candle in your heart, ready to be kindled.*
> *There is a void in your soul, ready to be filled.*
> *You feel it, don't you?*

Reflection Question

What narratives or self-talk keep you from trusting and believing that you are inherently worthy, regardless of your actions? Without judgment toward yourself or others, try to name how these developed within you.

_____

_____

_____

_____

_____

_____

Remember, according to Christian and Jewish tradition, God continuously announced that all of creation was not just worthy, but foundationally good! Regardless of the doings and actions of humanity, this ancient, sacred story grounds us in what Matthew Fox calls our "original blessing," an affirmation of our inherent and positive worth. If we can have the countercultural gumption to believe that, and to refuse to be neutral on a moving train, we can begin to live into that reality ourselves. That no matter what has been done to us by ourselves or others, we can claim our birthright and heritage: that we matter, we have worth, and we have inherent dignity simply for our act of *being*.

ACTION PROMPT

Who is one person in your community spheres of influence who might struggle with their sense of self-worth? After you identify the sphere of influence they're in and who they are, brainstorm how you might authentically affirm their inherent worthiness. What might that look like, sound like, and feel like, for both you and them?

Who: _____

How: _____

_____

_____

_____

_____

BODY PRACTICE:
THE SELF-WORTH MANTRA

Using the streaming service of your choice, listen to the song "Be Where You Are" by Birdtalker. As you listen mindfully, let each word sink into you. Allow your body to respond in whatever way it needs to. Feel free to dance if that's what your body wants!

As the song ends, find a comfortable place to sit quietly for about five minutes. Slowly introduce the following statement as a form of mantra for yourself during this time:

No matter what I have done or haven't done, I am enough.

This is meant to be an anchor phrase to take with you into your daily life. Whenever you find yourself feeling unworthy, inadequate, or conflicted about where your true value comes from, speak these words slowly and softly to yourself.

To remind you of this practice, one that is meant to be repeated in your day-to-day as needed, I recommend you write these words down on a piece of paper and carry it with you in your pocket. As time goes on and the words become a part of you, you can instead carry a small object such as a small stone to remind you to speak these words to yourself.

CHAPTER SEVEN

Constriction VI:
I am not in control.

Growing up, I was taught by my family that when I saw a problem, it was my duty to try to fix it. I was raised from a young age to be an active agent of change and justice, and while it was never said out loud, one of the implications I drew from this was that I had the power to save the world; I internalized the belief that it was mine to save.

This fit nicely with the message I was receiving from the larger culture around me as well. As a person with a white body, I was being taught through television and movies to view myself, much like Sean Connery in *Finding Forrester*, as a savior for people whose skin did not match the color of my own. As a boy and then a man, I was taught that my biological sex somehow bestowed upon me the role of protector of all women and non-binary people. As a person growing up Christian with the mission of "transforming the world," I was taught the world was inherently flawed and that only by my actions would it be changed to match the specific desires of my community. From all angles it was being ingrained in me, explicitly at times, that I had the power and duty to control the environment around me, all in the name of what was "best."

Reflection Question

In what circumstances or situations were you taught or expected to be in control? Who taught you this? How has it served you, both positively and negatively?

_____

_____

_____

_____

_____

_____

When I took my first teaching job, I took everything onto myself. I saw my classroom as the place I could prove myself; this would be the space in which I could transform the world. That brought with it both the good (a curriculum and a space centered on personal and community stories and social justice), and also the deeply problematic: the sense there was something wrong with the world to begin with and that it was mine to mold in my own image.

I became a building representative for my local union, which bolstered me even more as the "good protector" of the people. And when a new principal showed up and we didn't see eye to eye, I immediately felt as if I were in a holy war. Every day as I walked into the school building, my body carried the tension of being in an epic battle of good versus evil. Over the course of two years, this tension led to an ever-present, internal, bubbling anger and the feeling I was bashing my head against a wall over and over again.

Of course, in an emotional state of stress like this, other things in my life started to slip as well. My relationship with my then-fiancée, which had felt rock-solid, began to fall apart, turning my home into an extension of the war zone. I would come home from a day of battle and immediately transition to walking on tiptoes, actively working to avoid the landmines of saying or doing the "wrong thing."

It was in the midst of these two mountains of the unsolvable that I came face-to-face with the reality that I felt out of control. This was a situation I couldn't fix with a snap of my fingers or any amount of kind words. I began to feel my body and emotional life constricting within me, my understanding of the world perpetually twisting itself until nothing, not even my own experience, seemed for certain.

I remember clearly the night when the dam broke open in me. My partner and I were in an argument at home over something or other and I finally lost it. Tapping into the all-consuming anger present within me, mostly directed at myself, I hopped on my bike and all I could do was ride, my feet demanding the tires go faster with each push of the pedals. I later referred to this moment with my friends as my "Ride of Rage." My brain simply couldn't comprehend what was happening and my body had finally had enough of the stress and repression of emotions. I rode down the darkened streets at full speed as I pushed myself and angered at the world; it was only when my legs began to give and I came to a stop and just breathed that I was able to recognize for the first time the illusion I had been living in.

Richard Rohr often teaches that to feel "out of control" is as good a definition as we have for the act and experience of suffering. And because of this, he says, when we go through the suffering process, of feeling out of control, it can be the "most effective way whereby humans learn to trust, allow, and give up control to another source." And while he says he wishes there were another way, he teaches that this seems to be the "path and the price of full transformation into the divine."[14]

Have you ever noticed this suffering only continues and perpetuates even more suffering when we try to maintain our sense of control? It seems every attempt we make to remain in control over anything or anyone further tightens the constriction within us, severing us more and more from our awareness of our true selves. When we finally learn to unclench our fists and let go of our false sense of control, we can begin to let another source hold us. This is the nature of reality according to James Finley: the divine "protects us from nothing even as it sustains us in all things."[15] (Take a moment to read that again and see how you may have felt this in your own life!)

In the events that led up to my Ride of Rage, I recognize now that I was attempting to control my own inner life, repressing my emotions all the while trying to control everything outside of me as well. It was only through this experience of breaking that I was finally able to see it for what it was and begin to let go of *some* of my need for control. Nowadays, whenever I realize I have been clenching my jaw or my shoulders, I ask myself, "What have I been trying to control?" And more times than not, the answer appears fairly quickly.

Reflection Questions

What bodily sensations arise in you when you're attempting to be in control? Do you clench your teeth, hunch your shoulders, puff out your chest, or do something else? How do these bodily actions differ from when you are relaxed and calm?

_____

_____

_____

_____

_____

_____

How do you interact with others when you're attempting to be in control? How does this impact your relationships with them?

_____

_____

_____

_____

_____

_____

Residing in a world filled with uncertainties, unpleasantness, injustice, and brutality, we can be tempted to try to control all of it or to explain it away. And yet our wisdom teachers do not recommend attempting to control or bypass any of life's frailties. Instead, they invite us to more fully experience each one for what it is. Mirabai Starr, in words only she can conjure, writes, "Our loved ones did not die because we required a wake-up call. Our marriages do not go up in flames as a result of our pesky little attachments. We do not endure sexual abuse and institutional oppression on account of our dualistic preconceptions. Shit happens."[16]

When Rohr speaks of giving up control, he is teaching a practice of expansion: the act of letting go of all need for control in the first place. Instead of seeking to control or bypass the "shit" that's happening, a person practicing expansion will seek to recognize it, sit with it, and respond to it with compassion. Their response to the chaos of the world will not be "How can I tame this?" but rather, "It is what it is, and how can I be present with it in a loving way?"

In order to participate in the world around us rooted in our true selves, we need to develop an individual and communal approach to life's chaos that has the power to hold it gently: "It is what it is, and how can I be present with it in a loving way?" Rather than being another form of bypassing, this question invites us to see each moment clearly and respond intimately in ways that radiate love, rather than with a need to fix, save, advise, or control.

When I first introduced this in a workshop years ago, one participant asked me if I felt that this question promoted complacency and acceptance of the status quo. I paused for a moment before explaining that I think this question leads to the complete opposite. So much of the way our current activism in the world works is through antagonistic "conquer-or-be-conquered" energy; we experience something we see as wrong and immediately seek to destroy it. See problem, stop problem. And yet, this kind of activism is reactionary, always predated by the problem to begin with; it is an approach of annihilation, rather than reconciliation.

Instead, this question invites us to become close acquaintances with the problem, accepting that it is at work in our world for reasons that are bigger than the most visible symptom in front of us. From this place of acceptance and clear-eyed focus, we can then begin to work *with* it in a loving way to form a solution, not only to the current manifestation, but also in a way that can heal the roots of the problem. In other words, this question guides us to remember Thomas Merton's teaching of the spring and the stream. For our outer life to be empathetic, sustainable, and justice-oriented, our inner life must be tended to, fully present, and engaged.

Here's an example from the teaching world: when a high school student is acting out, by yelling abusive words at a teacher or perhaps even by bringing a knife to school in their backpack, the immediate response we've had for the past fifty years is to suspend or expel the kid. This is the response that comes from a control-focused, antagonistic, reactionary approach to problem-solving; by doing this, the student's behavior is removed from the school and the student receives a firm punishment. However, from years of sociological studies and broad recognition of the school-to-prison pipeline, we know this approach doesn't work long-term, for the student or for the community at large. It doesn't solve the problem; it just relocates it. Instead, entering into this problem with a reconciliatory energy—it is what it is, and how can I be present with it in a loving way?—leads the teachers and administrative staff to ask the question: why? After ending the immediate issue (removing the student from class or removing the weapon from the student), this approach leads to teachers sitting down with the student and seeking to understand the student. What is going on in that student's life that has led them to make the decisions they've made? How can we help to change those issues so that healing occurs and future problems are avoided? What boundaries need to be put in place for that student to feel safe and cared for?

The same is true within ourselves! When we experience something in our life that triggers us to feel out of control, how can we slow down, saying to ourselves, "It is what it is, and how can I be present with it in a loving way?" Perhaps this is an outward incident like a bad driver or frustrating family member or maybe even an inner emotion, like the roaring charge of anger that might show up when we feel out of control. The point is, this question invites us to be gentler with ourselves and our world, but no less actively engaged. By leaning into this invitation, we develop our capacity to hold great pain and suffering along with hope and curiosity, learning to see our world with soft eyes.

ACTION PROMPT

Scenario: Walking down a main road in your city or town, you see up ahead of you a man sitting on the sidewalk, asking people for spare change. He looks tired and as if he might be experiencing homelessness or food insecurity.

Brainstorm: Think about ways in which you might relationally respond to the situation in a way that honors the man's inherent dignity and is rooted in the teaching, "It is what it is, and how can I be present with it in a loving way?"

What can you say?

_____

_____

_____

_____

What can you do?

_____

_____

_____

_____

BODY PRACTICE:
RECOGNITION AND ACTION

As you begin this practice, attempt to set aside, if even for a moment, any need to fix, save, or change the world. This practice is focused on beginning to shift _how_ we see the world, not _what_ we see.

With a pen or pencil in hand, write down the following question in the center of a piece of paper and then circle it:

It is what it is, and how can I be present with it in a loving way?

These are the words we will come back to again and again during this exercise. We'll call it our "anchor question."

Around this question, go ahead and list everything in your life or in the world around you that you feel a lack of control over. (In the teaching world, we call this a brain dump.) These can be as large as climate change and as small as your wakeup time. Nothing you list is too big or too small.

After you have ten to twenty ideas listed, give yourself a moment to pause and review what you've written. Hopefully your list contains a good mix of both personal and societal items. (If not, that's okay!)

Now, pick one of the things you've listed to start with. Looking at your words, think about why you feel out of control in this instance.

With this in mind, say to yourself, "It is what it is." Recognize that in this moment, there is nothing you can do to fix or control it. You are simply attempting to non-judgmentally observe it—this is a thing that exists in the world and in your life. Repeat this phrase several times, seeking to come to some form of inner peace around its existence.

When you feel like you've recognized its existence without immediate judgment, ask yourself the next line of our anchor question, "How can I be present with it in a loving way?" Notice that this isn't an invitation for you to fix or control the issue, but rather to be present with it in a loving way. Spend a few minutes brainstorming in your head or on the paper; what would it look like for you to be present with this issue in a loving way? Not trying to demolish or eradicate it with power, but rather to bring your loving presence alongside it?

If any new idea, inspiration, or awakening comes to you, be sure to write it down. Step away from your paper and reflect on this. Create an action plan or an intention around this issue, if needed.

When you feel ready, preferably after a few hours or even days, come back to your paper and repeat this process again with another item you've listed.

For a guided version of this practice, visit the companion course.

CHAPTER EIGHT

Constriction VII:
I am not free.

An interesting conversation began to seep into daily life within American culture in the first half of 2021. As COVID-19 vaccines started to roll out across the United States, there was an explosion of questions around what would come next. When would businesses be free to open completely, as they had before the pandemic? When would we be able to forego our facemasks outside our homes? How would we know who is vaccinated and who is not? Who could we have in our homes and who would we need to keep our distance from for a while longer?

This conversation, necessitated by the realities of a slower-than-we-wanted vaccine rollout, continued to show the rips, tears, and scars in our American fabric. Communities began to boil from within as different people, including family members and friends, expressed their own tolerances for risk, opinions on the latest scientific findings, and willingness to quickly return to some form of "normal." In the midst of this conversation came ideas like vaccine passports, mandated vaccinations, and vaccinated-only sections at sports events, all ideas meant to limit the spread of COVID and get businesses to fully reopen. However, the implications of these ideas and the very concept of mandating personal health decisions (like had been done with other vaccines throughout our history) caused many people, from across the political spectrum, to question one of the fundamental tenets of American capitalism: what is freedom?

For many Americans, myself included, we have been brought up to respect and honor individual freedom. In fact, it wasn't until I was in my adult years that I learned any other form of freedom existed! For me, being free meant being able to do what I wanted without undue restriction, buy whatever I wanted given I had the money, and lead a life however I could, given my circumstances. In other words, freedom meant "I get to do what I want; if you try to stop me, you're the problem!" Based on the larger debate in the United States around freedom, I'm clearly not the only one with that original definition.

Reflection Question

Take a moment to think about your own definition of freedom. What were you taught about freedom? Today and in your own life, how do you experience freedom?

_____

_____

_____

_____

_____

And yet, that was never the only definition and understanding of freedom! Even mixed into my original understanding of freedom is the recognition that all of my personal freedom ("I can buy what I want . . .") is enclosed within the confines of a *lack* of structural freedom (". . . given I have the money.") Because of this, I was taught to be okay with being structurally unfree within capitalism as long as I felt personally free to do what I wanted, given those restrictions.

For people of color, women, those with disabilities, and those in the LGBTQ community, this conflicting reality is exponentially more visceral as structural racism, patriarchy, ableism, dualism, and heteronormativity intersect with capitalism to compound the damage of living in a confining system preaching a gospel of personal freedom. We are each being sold an idea of personal freedom that just isn't that free.

In fact, within this larger systematic context, our sense of personal freedom can begin to look quite small! The following model, based on the work by Brian McLaren, represents the shape of this societal reality.[17]

How can anyone claim to be free within systems and structures that are built to control our behaviors and ways of life?

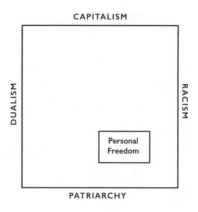

If this seems like a tenuous and potentially unstable form of freedom, *you're right.* It is. No wonder so many of us find ourselves constricting from within and defending our "freedom," challenging anyone who we perceive might be attempting to take it away. If we're already constrained within intersecting oppressive systems, it can seem only natural to grasp what little sense of certainty we have and wield it like a sword, defending ourselves from every perceived threat. (Especially if that perceived threat might destabilize our sense of belonging within a community!) We've been taught to build our identity and live within the illusion that we are free so that we don't question the structures that continue to surround and lay claim to us. Anything that then challenges our free identity threatens to crumble our entire worldview.

I once had a high school student who would come to school early every morning, sneaking into the building if he could, and sit on the bathroom floor until his first class started. Knowing this behavior drew suspicion from his teachers and other students, he would shut the door so that nobody knew he was there unless they came in. The principal of our school thought it was a bit abnormal and potentially a problem should we ever need to go into lockdown, so she called him into the office one day for a chat. Faced with the possible removal of his "morning space," he sat calmly in her presence, but the moment he got to my class, he went off about how cruel and unjust she was for even bringing it up. For the rest of the year, she was on his bad side, as he railed against her at every turn. Being a new principal, she didn't know what many of us who had taught him for years knew: his behavior was a survival technique. This student had an unstable homelife filled with emotional abuse, poverty, and food insecurity; he never felt safe anywhere. We had seen different symptoms of this in our classrooms, and so we knew this was his way of finding a sense of personal freedom and safety within the context of his structural constraints and chaos. When the principal challenged his access to that personal freedom, his supercharged reaction was an attempt to defend it.

Activity

In our modern world, various societal structures exist that provide benefit to some while, at the same time, causing harm to us all. In this activity, take some time to investigate their presence in your life and determine how each of these structures has caused you harm in the past or continues to have an impact on you today. Which structures do you reject, deny, or fight against? Which do you freely accept? (This is by no means an exhaustive list; it's just a place to start. If any of these are new terms for you, take a moment to look them up!)

Ableism

Capitalism/Economic Privilege

Cisgender Privilege

Couple/Partnership Privilege

Dualism

_____

_____

Educational Privilege

_____

_____

Geographical Privilege

_____

_____

Gender Identity Privilege

_____

_____

Heteronormativity

_____

_____

Patriarchy/Sexism

_____

_____

Racism/White Privilege

_____

_____

Religious Privilege

_____

_____

The great wisdom teachers were just like us in so many
ways, and they, too, were caught within structures that
kept them "under control and in line." (And to be sure,
some structures are useful; I like living within a society
where we have shared understandings of where to drive
on the road, for example.) Teresa of Ávila butted heads
with the Spanish patriarchy, Howard Thurman navigated
and challenged American racism, and Thich Nhat Hanh
was exiled from his home by his militaristic government
for more than forty years. In their attempts to understand

how to live meaningful lives within those structures, many of them came to an experience of a kind of freedom that is both bigger than personal and structural freedom and, at the same time, smaller and more deeply intimate.

This experience of freedom for them each came from their inner space, the place deep within them that had the power to embolden them through the ups and downs of life. We might call this authentic freedom or inner freedom. For Thurman, it was the sustaining power of the sound of the genuine within him. For Thomas Merton, it was the glowing beauty of his true self. It is the kind of freedom that sustained Viktor Frankl during his time in the Nazi concentration camps of World War II and Yuri Kochiyama as she fought for justice on the streets of the United States.

Pope Francis spoke during the pandemic of how we often touch upon authentic freedom in the midst of crisis. He writes, "In every personal 'COVID,' so to speak, in every 'stoppage,' what is revealed is what needs to change: our lack of internal freedom, the idols we have been serving, the ideologies we have tried to live by, the relationships we have neglected."[18] In order to live out of a true, authentic freedom, we must first set aside and let go of (or be stripped of) the masks we wear and our illusions about who we are and the way the world is—the very things keeping us *from* freedom.

Reflection Question

What masks and illusions are you holding on to in this stage of your life? How are they benefiting you? How are they hindering you or holding you captive?

_____

_____

_____

_____

_____

It will always be more comfortable, for a time, to hold on to our manufactured personality, which protects us. This is why it is so often not our own doing when the mask is removed, whether it be a result of a messy breakup, experiencing or witnessing police brutality, or having a moment of self-clarity in the context of struggle. No matter how it happens, the experience of authentic freedom comes when we are able to recognize the structural constraints that have been built around us and the illusion of personal freedom we have been holding tightly to. It comes when we feel and accept the constriction of "not being free" and then opt to embody our true self, reclaiming a deeper and more true sense of freedom.

When I talk about expanding through each of our constrictions, this is exactly what I'm talking about! When we touch upon this authentic freedom within ourselves, it feels like expansion! It feels like letting go of that which tethers us, taking a deep breath, and spreading our arms wide. It is not easily accessed under the cloaks of our societal and personal narratives, but when it is, it shines forth through our behaviors and our actions in the world. This is why our friends and family often notice our transformations, or expansions, even before we can! It is a freedom that does not shield us from the constraints of the world, but allows for our love to overflow abundantly into it.

Leaning into authentic freedom requires us to first open our eyes to the structures of power in the world and the posture we carry in it; only then can we shift our understanding of freedom from "I can do what I want" to "I can do what love draws me to do" to "I can be who love draws me to be."

ACTION PROMPT

Think about your community spheres of influence. What structural boundaries or barriers might be present in those spaces? What can you do this week to help reduce or eliminate the negative impacts of those structures?

Community Sphere(s) of Influence:

_____

Structural boundaries/barriers that still exist:

_____

_____

_____

Ways I can reduce or eliminate negative impacts:

_____

_____

_____

BODY PRACTICE: BREATH READING

Before beginning the Body Practice, I invite you to read the words of the following poem by Kahlil Gibran slowly to yourself. As you read, think about what you feel constrained by, both in your own internal narratives as well as the larger structures of society. What would it feel like to let those narratives go? What would it feel like in your body? What would it feel like to approach the structures of society that oppress and repress with an expansive heart of love, challenging them to give way? What would that expansiveness feel like?

> *But you, children of space, you restless in rest, you shall not be trapped nor tamed.*
>
> *Your house shall be not an anchor but a mast.*
>
> *It shall not be a glistening film that covers a wound, but an eyelid that guards the eye.*
>
> *You shall not fold your wings that you may pass through doors, nor bend your heads that they strike not against a ceiling, nor fear to breathe lest walls should crack and fall down.*
>
> *You shall not dwell in tombs made by the dead for the living.*

And though of magnificence and splendor, your house shall not hold your secret nor shelter your longing.

For that which is boundless in you abides in the mansion of the sky, whose door is the morning mist, and whose windows are the songs and the silences of night.[19]

After you have read it once, take a moment in reflection. When you're ready, read the poem again. This time, as you read each line, inhale or exhale as the words wash over you. Go back and forth, inhaling and exhaling with the words, for the entirety of the poem.

When you finish reading, hold that silence for a few moments, reflecting on "that which is boundless in you." (You may find it helpful to also extend your arms to the side and up with each inhale, followed by returning them back down with each exhale.)

For a guided version of this practice, visit the companion course.

CHAPTER NINE

Constriction VIII:
I am my trauma.

The process of unmasking ourselves is almost always a terrifying endeavor, whether it is undertaken of our own free will or foisted upon us by what seems a cruel and painful world. Being forced to look into the mirror and recognize that the "you" you see yourself as isn't your full and complete true self is an act of dying. In that moment of recognition, there is a part of ourselves that splinters and begins to fade into the background. When we choose to let go of that mask, we're trusting there is something on the other side of that small death.

When we see our true identities unprotected, even if just for a moment before covering ourselves up again, there is a great risk being taken. When we see under our masks, many of us will begin to see our trauma in a new way: the traumas we encountered as children or as adults, or those we've done to ourselves, or those done by the hands and words of others. Each of us carries the scars of trauma in our lives; that's why we create such firm personalities to protect us! And so this unmasking can itself cause more trauma, or reignite the traumas we're already carrying with us, as the illusion we live in reluctantly gives way.

Oftentimes, when done best, this is a process that is guided by a deep soul friend, mental health professional, or healthy spiritual director; this is someone who can walk alongside us as we journey into ourselves. They can help us continue to take our mask off when we get scared, reminding us that we are not alone, or they can cheer us on when we inevitably think about holding on to the illusion. In fact, and obvious to some of us despite the vulnerability it requires, this entire process is perhaps *best* done within a community of trust, even though so much of it is solo work; as humans, we seem to need others around us to help us process and understand better the truth of who we are. Scientist and theologian Pierre Teilhard de Chardin is said to have once taught, "We are not human beings having a spiritual experience. We are spiritual beings having a human experience." This "human experience" seems often to require our personal growth to be contextualized within a community.

Reflection Question

Who in your life would you consider part of your community of trust?

_____

_____

_____

_____

_____

_____

And yet, even with the best of soul friends and supportive community, it remains deeply challenging; facing reality and the uncertain results of necessary change is tremendously difficult. There's a reason Neo paused for so long when faced with the decision of taking the red pill or the blue pill in *The Matrix*. The choice itself to stray further from the safety of our illusions is an act of bravery, placing our trust in something bigger than ourselves.

In my own life, I've had to come to grips with my own trauma around my body image. When I was young, I was fat-shamed by my friends and those around me, sometimes for having "cankles" and at other times simply for having a larger body. For someone who considered himself an athlete, this often felt like a fate worse than death. The deep shame and guilt I carried manifested itself in almost every facet of my life. I would wear clothes two or three sizes too large, fat-shame myself before others could do it to me, amplify my humor in an attempt to show my value, and rebel in the ways I could. My deep shame that I wasn't good enough, fit enough, or lovable enough led me to "cast my net wide" in terms of friends. Before long I was cutting classes to smoke weed at the nearby park, supplying the alcohol for our high school parties, and generally flirting with anyone who would laugh at my jokes. I felt ashamed of my body, so I tried to make up for it in any way I could.

By the time I got to college, my body had become taller and I was no longer made fun of for my weight and size, but this new development was largely irrelevant. My personality, my mask, however outdated, still led me to live in a world where I felt fat and unwanted.

At university, I fell into a great group of friends, each of us sharing a similar experience. We began to refer to ourselves as the "Former Fat Kids Club," a collection of young men who had a common story growing up feeling overweight and ashamed because of our bodies. I'll never forget the wondrous joy I experienced when I learned that all of us had memories of tiptoeing down the hallways of our childhood homes late at night, bags of Lay's potato chips carefully hanging from our fingertips so that no one would hear them crinkle as we made our way to our beds. I had found my people!

As I look back at this moment in my life, I recognize another truth: as my initial mask of being the funny fat kid began to slip off in college, I had so identified with my trauma that I remade a new one that could continue to protect me; I became a Former Fat Kid. I was unable, at that time, to simply let go of my trauma; I simply didn't have the tools. I had no concept of the truth that I would later hear from James Finley, echoing the words of Carl Jung: "You are not what has been done to you." And so I lived with the constriction of "I am my trauma," thus creating new ways to protect myself from my own pain and shame.

Sometimes when we enter into the unmasking process and face our trauma, we can end up molding ourselves new personalities based solely on that trauma all over again. This identification with our trauma, creating a personality out of it, is a way to make sense of it, taking back power, connecting with others who have shared experience. For me, becoming part of the Former Fat Kids Club was just that! It was powerful *and* further constricting within me. It gave me a beautiful community while also allowing me to retain my identification with the victimhood of my experience. If I had been left in this space for long, of identification with my trauma and with victimhood, I believe I would have been just as unhealthy as before. But I wasn't; being in this group of friends allowed me to begin to grow. In a community of shared experience, I was able to slowly emerge from my own shell of shame and learn to take pride in myself, knowing I wasn't alone.

Reflection Question

Think about the traumas you have experienced in your life, both big and small. (Take your time and lean on your community of trust, if needed!) How do you relate with these experiences? How have you possibly identified with your trauma, wrapping it into your personality?

_____

_____

_____

_____

_____

_____

Slowly but surely, this constriction softened within me, shifting from "I am my trauma" to "I am traumatized" to "I am traumatized, *and* ..."

This word, *and*, might be the most important word in this context because it speaks to the realities that our identity and our trauma are not the same things and that each of us can live with a constriction *and* grow through it. It seems almost like a necessary requirement for expansion that we notice how our personal identities are different from the traumas we have experienced. While our traumas have certainly shaped our personalities, the essence of our identity is something else entirely. Rev. angel Kyodo williams writes that "if we are to heal, then we must allow our awareness to settle into and integrate with the pain and discomfort that has been habitually avoided."[20] We cannot bypass our pain or shame or feelings of guilt and inadequacy, but we can bring our loving awareness to these experiences and begin to grow and expand through them. For me, this has meant embracing compassion for myself and, at the same time, learning to have more compassion for others' traumas, whatever they may be. Entering into my own experience of life, filled with its complexities, hurts, and joys, has helped me become more attuned to the experiences of others around me, especially of my students.

Rumi writes that the "wound is the place where the Light enters you." That wounding is inevitable *and* that each wound is a passageway for transformation is one of the great spiritual truths of life. This is why it is so important to have a good therapist, spiritual director, or soul friend: someone who can walk with us in the paradoxical space of exploring our wounds so that we can find a way through them. The work of expanding through this constriction is to lean more and more into the *and*, learning how to hold the tension of our own pain and beautiful possibility.

ACTION PROMPT

Think about an upcoming meeting or situation that might be tense or difficult. What are one or two things you can do to emanate love in that space, knowing that others are also filled with their own complexities and traumas?

Situation:

_____

_____

_____

Why might this situation be tense or difficult?

_____

_____

_____

_____

What can you do to emanate love in this space?

_____

_____

_____

_____

BODY PRACTICE:
MUSCLE CLENCHING RELAXATION PRACTICE

This is a physical practice of letting go, but it works similarly with our internal life; we often clench and cling to our ideas, thoughts, emotions, histories, and what we think makes us "us." During this exercise, you might want to imagine letting go of your stress or certain ideas or traumatic experiences you have felt attached to.

Sitting or standing, allow your arms to rest either in your lap or by your sides. Take two or three deep breaths as your eyes gently close.

Slowly wiggle each of your fingers, becoming aware of the sensation of each of their movements. Then, begin to tighten your hands into the form of fists. Feel yourself clenching as hard as you can and holding that clench for five seconds before releasing softly. Feel how each of your muscles relaxes and come to a new and calm equilibrium. Repeat this two or three times.

This practice can also be effective when done with shoulders, forearms, glutes, quads, calves, and feet.

For a guided version of this practice, visit the companion course.

CHAPTER TEN

Constriction IX:
I do not know who I am.

As a high school teacher, I am intimately aware of how prevalent this constriction is in young people between the ages of fourteen and eighteen. Working with teenagers is amazing for many reasons, but my favorite aspect of the work is that I get to mentor and walk alongside kids as they constantly negotiate and renegotiate who they are and who they want to be. There is not a single twelfth grader who graduates as the same person as they were in ninth grade; they have been changed by their friends, by content in school, by good and bad experiences, and hopefully by one or two caring and supportive teachers. This is a constriction that almost everyone feels at least once in their lives, which makes it the perfect one for us to end with. In many ways, this small book seeks to help us cope with and move through this final constriction by way of each of the other constrictions.

Our culture seems to celebrate this idea of "not knowing" in teenagers, but then never again as we age. In teenagers, it is seen as the great and positive coming of age process, but in adults it is most often seen negatively as a mid-life crisis or marked by behavior labeled aimless, shiftless, or unfocused. By placing such a negative stigma on not knowing who we are, American culture disincentivizes us from ever showing this outwardly, despite it being experienced by universally everyone at some point. American culture does not do well with the uncontrollable, and this constriction is most certainly that; it is the basis of great chaos and great possibility.

It was into this mysterious in-between space that I flung myself a few years ago. Burned out by teaching and exhausted by the end of a major relationship, I uprooted myself in just about every way I could—I quit my job as a teacher, said goodbye to my friends and the city I lived in, and moved into a house shared between five tenants, two partners, and a dog named Effie. (To this day, I am endlessly thankful for the circumstances and economic privileges that allowed me to do this; I am also thankful to no longer be living in that house with the constant smell of weed floating through the kitchen.)

While much of this decision was based in burnout, the truth is that I had lost contact with who I was. So much of my identity had been wrapped up in being a great teacher, a great partner, and an optimistic change agent in the world, and when my masks slipped off, I felt as if I were entirely rudderless and falling into the unknown.

As we've already explored repeatedly, we very rarely let our guard down enough to go completely maskless. This is why this process is so traumatic; it doesn't happen often! But it's also traumatic because it is identity-shattering. Whether it first happens in life as a teenager, during a layoff from work as an adult, or following the death of a loved one, it seems to be the same. During any instance of disillusionment, there is an unusual and momentary masklessness in which the mysterious unknown becomes uncomfortably real. When we experience a true unmasking experience, we will almost inevitably feel the constriction of "I don't know who I am," which is already ever present in so many of us, tightening even further. I know I certainly did.

Reflection Question

When is a time in your life you've felt disillusioned or in this mysterious unknown? What was your response to this feeling? What new insights were awakened during this experience?

_____

_____

_____

_____

_____

_____

In my opinion, one of the greatest awakenings in the West of the past one hundred years is the unearthing and recovering of the Christian contemplative tradition. With its emphasis on silence, inner questioning, and embracing of the unknown, it provides language for so many of us in conflict with traditional religious teaching, with which to explore the meaning of our lives deeper. In a strange way, it has reopened me to exploring sacred stories to find whatever truth might lie within them.

In the Christian scriptures, for example, there is a painful and infinitely relatable moment that speaks into this moment of not knowing exactly who we are (and in this case, why our behaviors are what they are):

> I do not understand my own behavior; I do not act as I mean to, but I do things that I hate . . . for though the will to do what is good is in me, the power to do it is not: the good thing I want to do, I never do; the evil thing which I do not want—that is what I do.[21]

You can almost hear the writer of this passage shaking their head toward the ground and letting out a deep sigh of anguish. The realization that we aren't entirely sure of who we are, and why in the world we're going about our lives in the way we are, is exhausting!

Reflection Question

How have you experienced this misalignment between your ideals and your own behaviors in your life? What does this feel like in your body? How has it impacted the way in which you engage the world around you?

_____

_____

_____

_____

Again, it really seems that becoming disillusioned and entering the unknown is necessary! In almost every spiritual tradition, there is a similar trajectory for spiritual and personal growth: search for attainment, recognition of the limitations of attainment and attachment, letting go, and experience of and connection into divinity, whatever name you might have for it. Richard Rohr and Pema Chodron teach this through emphasizing the importance of failing, letting go, and change in the process of growing up and spiritually maturing. In spiritual and emotional work with men, the phrase that is often used is "tower building": the process by which each of us develops our sense of self through work, climbing ladders, and achievement. Only when we realize the limitations and illusions of self-determination, and often as we experience the natural failings and reflections brought about by old age, do we then enter the unknown and begin to take the tower apart and recognize it is no longer needed. This process is often known as the path of descent; it seems we usually need to experience the struggles of life (and our constrictions) in order to let go of what we once held dear and begin to experience full expansion.

Scattered throughout this book are different words and ideas and phrases for what it means to experience the expansiveness of ultimate reality, to fully and completely understand who we are in the context of our interconnected universe. Thomas Merton referred to our own expansion as finding and becoming in contact with our true self, which is our internal and immortal connection with the divine. Howard Thurman spoke of us hearing the "sound of the genuine" emanating from within us and overflowing from others around us. Others have named our identity as being part of the great web of being or have spoken of our inherent love-nature.

These are all attempts at explaining and naming "who we are," both as individuals and as a collective people. In a society where we are being bombarded by voices trying to tell us who we are (and sell us new identities), these voices give a clear and yet uneasy response: we are inherently good, connected to That Which Is Bigger Than Us, and, in Neil deGrasse Tyson's words, "in kinship with all life on Earth."

These wisdom teachers proclaim we each carry divine DNA inside us; we are not simply physical beings but rather, to again quote Pierre Teilhard de Chardin, "spiritual beings having a human experience." Expanding beyond our masked and constricted selves will require allowing ourselves to fall into the unknown, making the absurd decision to place our trust in the possibility that this might just be true.

BODY PRACTICES FOR EXPANSION

Rather than just one Body Practice to end this chapter, what follows are several that have helped me, and continue to help me, in my own expansion work. They can be used at any time to deepen your connection with your inner life or to help you refocus on your commitment to sustained activism in your outer life. I hope you may find something that connects with your heartspace, inviting you into this continual and never-ending work.

Wake Up: With a cup of coffee, tea, or hot chocolate, spend some time observing your life. Open a journal or the notes app on your phone, and reflect on each of the following questions. What masks have you worn in different settings to protect yourself? Which masks do you still wear the most often? What illusions have you experienced living in and recognizing? Which illusions might you still be living in? What keeps you from taking off your mask more often or from working to set aside these illusions?

Grow Up: Take a few moments to sit in silence or at the beach listening to the waves. Listen to your own body. Listen for the sound of the genuine. What does it feel like to listen for the sound of the genuine strumming from within you? What does it feel like to listen for the sound of the genuine strumming from within others?

Clean Up: Observing your life with soft, nonjudgmental eyes, what needs to change so that your values and behaviors are in alignment? What steps can you take this week to make small and healthy changes? What steps can you take in the next month to make bigger, more structural changes? Grab a piece of paper and write down a plan, placing it where you can see it each day this week!

Show Up: As you look into the world and your place in it, how are you radiating love within your spheres of influence? In what tangible ways are you supporting and affirming the dismantling of structures of injustice? How can you more fully show up as your true self through listening to, participating with, and standing up for the inherent dignity within yourself and others?

APPENDIX

Wisdom Teachers

Below are each of the wisdom teachers named in this book, as well as a few more who have been instrumental in my life. Along with a short note about each teacher, I'll include specific recommendations for books, podcasts, or articles to deepen in their teachings wherever possible.

angel Kyodo williams

A Zen Buddhist priest and activist, Rev. angel Kyodo williams has been vitally important in my life, helping me to dislodge the idea that my inner work is disconnected from the outer work of action, justice, and societal liberation. She is the co-author, along with Lama Rod Owens and Jasmine Syedullah, of an amazing book, *Radical Dharma: Talking Race, Love, and Liberation*.

Barbara Holmes

One of my teachers at the Living School for Action and Contemplation, Dr. B (as we lovingly call her) focuses her teaching on African American spirituality, mysticism, cosmology, and culture. Her most recent book, *Crisis Contemplation*, is a must-read for developing an embodied spirituality that can listen to and help heal a deeply hurting world.

Brian McLaren

A former evangelical Christian pastor, Brian McLaren is now a leading voice in the contemplative Christianity movement. He's written many books, but two of the most impactful on my life have been *The Great Spiritual Migration* and *Faith after Doubt*. I also highly recommend his podcast, *Learning How to See*. He is also one of my teachers at the Living School for Action and Contemplation.

Christena Cleveland

I first encountered Dr. Christena Cleveland when she spoke at a conference in Albuquerque on the topic of white supremacy and racism within Christian institutions. She is the founder of the Center for Justice + Renewal and a powerful voice for spiritual and social transformation. Her e-newsletter has been one of the most challenging and beautiful things I've subscribed to in recent years. You can find her at www.christenacleveland.com.

Evelyn Underhill

Evelyn Underhill was an English mystic, poet, and Christian theologian. One of her greatest contributions to the growing literature on mysticism is her book, *Mysticism*, an exploration of mystic experience within Christianity, Sufism, Hinduism, Buddhism, and other faith traditions.

Howard Thurman

Howard Thurman was at once a social activist, public theologian, mentor to Martin Luther King Jr., and an internally engaged mystic. If you're just hearing of him, I recommend two places to start: his book, *Jesus and the Disinherited*, and his commencement address at Spelman College. The latter can be found with a quick online search.

Jacqui Lewis

Rev. Jacqui Lewis is the senior minister of Middle Collegiate Church in New York and a powerful activist for racial, economic, and gender and sexuality justice. Her podcast, *Love. Period.*, is an amazing listen as she has conversations with others about what fierce love can look like both internally and outwardly in our world.

James Finley

We in the Living School refer to James Finley as Uncle Jim, a poetic, mystical powerhouse of vulnerability and authenticity. He was at one point a student of Thomas Merton before becoming a clinical psychologist, honoring both of these aspects of his past as he teaches. I recommend listening to his podcast *Turning to the Mystics,* where he provides meditations on the works of Teresa of Ávila, Thomas Merton, and John of the Cross, among others.

Jeffrey Moses

An expert in comparative religion, meditation, and spiritual development, Jeffrey Moses's book *Oneness* is one of the seminal texts for understanding the wisdom shared between many religions.

Julian of Norwich

The most celebrated English mystic of the fourteenth century, Julian of Norwich had many direct experiences of the divine throughout her life and communicated them in her book, *Revelations of Divine Love*. For an accessible version, I highly recommend Mirabai Starr's translation: *The Showings of Julian of Norwich*.

Ken Wilber

Possibly the most compelling yet challenging modern philosopher I've read, Ken Wilber has spent his life dedicated to developing a "theory of everything" that can explain the connection between different religious traditions, scientific findings, and philosophies. For a primer and general overview of his work, I recommend his book, *The Integral Vision*.

Kahlil Gibran

Best known as the author of *The Prophet*, Kahlil Gibran was a Lebanese poet, artist, and mystic. His work was highly influenced by his Christian upbringing, his proximity to Sufi mysticism, and Jungian psychology.

Mary Oliver

Although she probably would have fought against this title, I have again and again heard Mary Oliver referred to as Saint Mary Oliver in workshops and speeches. She is one of the deepest wells of wisdom in twentieth and twenty-first century poetry and a perfect example of eldership in modern society. My favorite book of hers is *Devotions: The Selected Poems of Mary Oliver*, released just two years before her death in 2019.

Matthew Fox

Expelled from the Catholic church for his feminist theology, interfaith work with Indigenous peoples, refusal to condemn homosexuality, and teaching on creation spirituality, Matthew Fox is one of the most influential theologians of the late twentieth century.

His book *Original Blessing* challenged the doctrine of original sin and has provided hundreds of thousands of Christians an alternative view of human dignity and divinity.

Mirabai Starr

Mirabai Starr is one of the most influential teachers in my life, helping me to encounter the feminine energy of the divine, both within me and outside of me. Her book, *Wild Mercy: Living the Fierce and Tender Wisdom of the Women Mystics*, is a masterpiece and a must-read. It remains one of the few books I have purchased repeatedly because I keep giving the book away.

Parker Palmer

I was first introduced to Parker Palmer's work through his writings on education and leadership, but soon found his to be a fount of wisdom in just about every subject matter. He is the founder of the Center for Courage & Renewal and author of many books, including my favorites, *The Active Life* and *The Courage to Teach*.

Pema Chodron

Pema Chodron is a Buddhist nun currently teaching at Gampo Abbey in Nova Scotia. Throughout her life, she has written and taught extensively on the principle of "shenpa" and the ways in which we can become stuck in patterns of negative thoughts and actions. Her book, *Fail, Fail Again, Fail Better*, is a fabulous primer on how we can shift our mindsets around what success looks like in order to lead happier lives.

Phileena Nikole

Phileena has been hugely impactful in my life through her books, online presence, and teachings. I met her a few years ago in passing and was quickly moved by her authenticity and ability to listen deeply. She co-founded Gravity, a Center for Contemplative Activism to support people in the bridging of their inner and outer lives and to teach contemplative practices.

Pierre Teilhard de Chardin

A Jesuit paleontologist, Pierre Teilhard de Chardin wrote deeply of the sacredness of matter, believing that the divine was infused within everything we see, touch, and experience. While many of his teachings were rejected by the Jesuit authorities of his time, his works are currently being reexamined and lifted up for the ways in which he saw connection between the scientific and the spiritual.

Pope Francis

Not much needs to be said here in the way of biography, so I'll just recommend his second encyclical, *Laudato Si: On Care for Our Common Home*. In it, he lays out the spiritual and moral imperative for taking care of our shared Earth.

Rainer Maria Rilke

Writing around the turn of the nineteenth century, Rainer Maria Rilke's poetry explored the nature of beauty alongside grief, suffering, pain, and death. In his poetry, he often speaks of God not as a formal deity but as more of a life force that runs throughout all of nature and living matter. One of my favorite poems by Rilke is "The Night."

Resmaa Menakem

Over the past five years, Resmaa Menakem has become one of my most intimate of wisdom teachers, helping me to understand my white body, the impact it has in our world, and the trauma it carries within it. His book, *My Grandmother's Hands: Racialized Trauma and the Pathway to Mending Our Hearts and Bodies*, reads like a gift of love for the world, challenging us, especially white people, to engage white supremacy, not as an intellectual concept, but in a fully embodied way.

Richard Rohr

Perhaps nobody has done more to affirm and deepen my spirituality than Richard Rohr, a Franciscan priest and the academic dean of the Living School for Action and Contemplation. Launching the Center for Action and Contemplation to create a space for people to integrate their inner life with social justice, his teachings on incarnational mysticism and contemplation have changed my life. I recommend starting with his book *Falling Upward* or listening to his podcast *Another Name for Every Thing*.

Rumi

When I first encountered the thirteenth century Sufi mystic Rumi, I remember breaking down in tears at the beauty of his words. Many of his metaphors and images crossed the vast barriers of culture and time and seemed to speak directly to my inner experience of the divine. His poetry on sorrow and joy continues to be a welcome companion in my life. Coleman Barks has a good translation of his work, titled *The Essential Rumi*.

Rupi Kaur

The youngest of the teachers on this list, I firmly believe Rupi Kaur's poetry belongs in our modern anthology of wisdom. Her poems beautifully and strikingly get to the core of what it means to be human, embracing the pain, sorrow, joy, and love of each and every moment. While all of her books are powerful, *Home Body* explores the role of the self, touching on themes of self-love, nature, and light and darkness.

Teresa of Ávila

Teresa of Ávila is one of my oldest spiritual teachers, being the first mystic whose words I fell in love with. I remember riding buses throughout Seattle, so fully engulfed in *The Interior Castle (translated by Mirabai Starr)*, that I would miss stops and have to walk for blocks to make up lost ground. She is a powerful guide for those looking for support in their own interior journeys.

Thelma Hall

Thelma Hall's book, *Too Deep for Words*, roots the practice of lectio divina, or divine reading, in the Christian scriptures, but more than this, it shows the theological underpinnings of contemplative spirituality within the Christian tradition. For those wondering how contemplative Christian spirituality connects with traditional theological orthodoxy, this is a wonderful little book to pick up.

Thich Nhat Hanh

Zen Master and peace activist Thich Nhat Hanh was once referred to by Dr. Martin Luther King Jr. as "an apostle of peace and nonviolence" before being nominated for the Nobel Peace Prize. His entire life has been dedicated to teaching mindfulness and bringing forth a global spiritual awakening that will lead to the end of hatred, oppression, and war. His book, *Living Buddha, Living Christ*, looks at the various teachings of Buddha and Jesus, seeking to bring the contemplative traditions of both Buddhism and Christianity into dialogue with each other.

Thomas Keating

If Thomas Merton recovered and reintroduced contemplative Christianity to the Christian community, it was Thomas Keating who found a way to apply it within normal everyday life. Along with two others, he developed Centering Prayer, a contemplative meditation practice for people to engage with. Centering Prayer is now taught around the world, and individuals and small groups using this practice can be found in nearly every city across the United States.

Thomas Merton

Thomas Merton is often credited with singlehandedly recovering the contemplative tradition within Christianity and making it accessible to people in our modern era. As he aged, he seemed to deepen in his own spiritual understanding while broadening to engage in interfaith dialogues around the world, experiencing and seeking to articulate a spirituality that flows beneath and beyond all cultural and political differences. His book, *New Seeds of Contemplation*, is considered a spiritual classic of the twentieth century.

Gratitudes

Writing this book has been something of a spiritual practice, giving me an outlet for sharing many of the lessons and learnings I've gathered from those around me in my life. I am eternally thankful for the love and support of my parents, Rich and Cathy, who got excited with me, helped me discern directions in which to go, and were always there when I called. Mom and Dad: you have been the closest of wisdom teachers for me, and I honor you with my every breath.

To my brother, Michael, who broke my basketball hoop when I was seven and who threw my bicycle down a hill when I was nine: thank you for teaching me great resilience in the face of adversity. You've shown me how to ask the big questions and get curious about life, and I'm so deeply grateful to be your brother. And I'm sorry for throwing that rock at you when we were younger.

I have the most heartfelt gratitude for all the spiritual companions and friends I've walked with along the way. To Josh, Jane, Michael, Eric, Whitney, Jenn, Ximena, Anders, Claire, Dan, Lily, James, Randall, Graham, and J: I have grown so much just by being next to you and learning to create and hold space with you.

To Meg, Ryan, Ernest, Stephen, Kelsey, Angelie, Lydia, and Steven: our time at the Living School together has deeply changed me, helping me to live more and more into who I truly am. Thank you all for the abundance of laughter and tears we have shared together.

To my dear friend and Elder, Molly Hoffman: you have shown me how to age with grace, to lead with openness, and to see the world with curiosity. You are not an Elder just because of your age, but because of the ways you have learned to look inward, honor each part of yourself (even your snark!), and to lovingly grow even further.

To Stan, Colleen, Sharis, and Tony: I can't possibly ignore the impact of living with neighbors as amazing as you all. You have sat with me in the depths of great sadness, laughed with me around the fire, drank to the joys of life, and lived good lives side by side.

I'm thankful for everyone at Wise Ink and the publishing team who helped this book come together. When I started this writing process, I told myself I would take it from start to finish; thank you all for helping my dream become a reality.

To all the baristas, bartenders, restaurant workers, and Airbnb hosts I've met in the past two years: thank you for your service, your space, your time, and your love. I couldn't have done this without you.

And finally, to my own wisdom teachers, living and deceased, I offer nothing but honor and absurd joy.

To Richard Rohr, Cynthia Bourgeault, Jim Finley, Barbara Holmes, Brian McLaren, angel Kyodo williams, Mirabai Starr, Teresa of Ávila, Howard Thurman, and so many more: I honor you.

To the people of the Duwamish and Puyallup Tribes, past, present, and future, on whose land I am writing and living my life: I honor you.

To the trees and the great bodies of water surrounding me: I honor you.

To my ancestors, both blood and spiritual, I honor you.

To my descendants, I honor you.

Notes

1 James A. Pearson, https://jamesapearson.com/.

2 Barbara Holmes, "Race and the Cosmos," 2020, Living School for Action and Contemplation.

3 Phileena Nikole, *Mindful Silence* (Downers Grove: InterVarsity Press, 2018), 16–17.

4 Jeffrey Moses, *Oneness* (New York: Ballantine Books, 2002), xi.

5 Birdtalker, "One," track 11 on *One*, streaming.

6 Matthew Fox, *Original Blessing* (Santa Fe: Bear and Co., 1983).

7 Pema Chodron, *Fail, Fail Again, Fail Better* (Boulder: Sounds True, 2015).

8 Mirabai Starr, *Wild Mercy* (Boulder: Sounds True, 2019), 159.

9 Rev. Dr. Jacqui Lewis, host, "An Introduction to Love. Period." *Love. Period.* (podcast), April 17, 2021.

10 Deja Thomas and Juliana Menasce Horowitz, "Support for Black Lives Matter has decreased since June but remains strong among Black Americans," Pew Research Center, September 16, 2020, https://www.pewresearch.org/fact-tank/2020/09/16/support-for-black-lives-matter-has-decreased-since-june-but-remains-strong-among-black-americans/.

11 *Cosmos: A Spacetime Odyssey*, season 1, episode 2. Directed by Brannon Braga and Ann Druyan. Aired March 16, 2014. Fox.

12 Resmaa Menakem, *My Grandmother's Hands* (Las Vegas: Central Recovery Press, 2017), 54–55.

13 Evelyn Underhill, *The Fruits of the Spirit* (Atlanta: Church Publishing, 1989).

14 Richard Rohr, *Things Hidden: Scripture as Spirituality* (Cincinnati: Franciscan Media: 2008), 24–25.

15 James Finley, *Intimacy: The Divine Ambush* (Center for Action and Contemplation: 2013), CD.

16 Starr, *Wild Mercy*, 45.

17 Brian McLaren, "What Is Progressive Christianity?" March 10, 2020, Living School for Action and Contemplation.

18 Pope Francis, *Let Us Dream: The Path to a Better Future* (New York: Simon & Schuster, 2020), 36.

19 Kahlil Gibran, *The Prophet* (New York: Knopf, 1973), 33–34.

20 Rev. angel Kyodo williams, *Radical Dharma* (Berkeley: North Atlantic Books, 2016), 64–65.

21 Romans 7:15, 18–19.

About the Author

Andrew Lang is an educator in the Pacific Northwest and an alumnus of the Living School for Action and Contemplation, led by Richard Rohr, Cynthia Bourgeault, James Finley, Barbara Holmes, and Brian McLaren. He facilitates workshops on contemplative and embodied spirituality and shadow work. You can find more of his writings and offerings at www.AndrewGLang.com.

Thank You for Reading!

Writing this book has been a labor of love for me, and I'm overjoyed that it has found its way into your hands.

Please take a moment and leave a review on Amazon letting folks know your favorite part or teaching, an insight you've had, or any other way this book has impacted you.

Thank you!